When Life Shakes You Up

... An on purpose faith response to crisis

KEN ARDREY

DEDICATION

To all those who have allowed me to serve as their pastor through the years. Special appreciation to friends and loved ones in the Fishkill Church of the Nazarene who showed such love, patience, and support when my life was shaken and I needed so much help from God's people.

To my loving and faithful wife Brenda and my family, Dave, Ryan, Jonathan, and Christina who are my greatest blessing in life, and whose lives have been shaken as well.

CONTENTS

INTRODUCTION

Life is not Fair

I was a late bloomer. It all started in 1955 as a five year old beginning first grade. This was back in the dark ages before kindergarten. Five and six year olds were herded into class rooms, sat in rows, and taught the three R's and other valuable life lessons. Not the least of which was the authority of teachers.

During the first two weeks I should have been in school, I was in the hospital fighting a rather stubborn infection. My friends spent those weeks learning the ropes of Farnsworth Elementary School. I arrived as a timid five year old, not even knowing there were ropes. I sat in the classroom scared and lost. Here I was, not far removed from my first steps, and I now found myself in the first of twenty consecutive years of education.

Mrs. Murphy was a short, stout and stern-looking woman who administered her classroom with an iron fist. The rules and directions were all new to me, and I ended up standing in the wrong line or committing some other serious infraction. I guess she wanted to make sure I knew who was boss because she grabbed my arm and shoved me into my rightful place. Every first grade child in those days was marked with the scab of the required small pox vaccination. Mrs. Murphy was careless enough, or sadistic enough, to grab on to my vaccination arm, opening the wound, which bled all down my arm. Somehow, this was my fault, and I was scolded roundly for it.

This day was not my finest hour. I was too scared of my new teacher to ask permission to use the boys' room, and the only alternative was to wet my pants. Again I was brought in front of the class, humiliated, and sent to "the office" on my first day of school. The memory fades of what happened in "the office," but I think water boarding was legal back then.

Early in life I learned that life wasn't fair ...and that "stuff" happens. I learned experientially that the "stuff" of life can really shake you up. These early experiences impacted me in a way that affected the next ten years of education (which is as good an excuse as any for poor grades). As a child I had no idea how to respond to my time of hurt and pain. Especially in those days, the teacher was always right. If I was in trouble at school, I was also in trouble at home. My response was withdrawal and underachievement. I was just too young and immature to have a strategy figured out.

Too often, even as adults, we have no strategy in our response to the crises of life. We are shocked and indignant that the cosmos would conspire against us in such a way. When hit with the hurt, the pain, and the unfairness of life, we are so unprepared that the response is panic, fear, anger, blame and depression. As we look at the crises of life that shake our foundations and overwhelm us with fear and doubt, we will ask a personal question: *How do you respond when life shakes you up?* This is an important question. As people of faith we need not rely upon the inadequate resource of self sufficiency. We can respond with faith, "on purpose," to whatever life brings our way. The events of my life have challenged me to respond with faith in ways I never expected. My hope is that God's grace at work in the challenges of my situation will be used as a help and encouragement to others.

Personal

I was a late bloomer in sports as well. Being one of the smallest in all my classes was not an advantage in my athletic endeavors. Entering into the sophomore year of high school, I was all of 5' 0" tall. The teacher stopped me in the hallway to begin extradition proceedings back to junior high. God did answer prayer, and by faith and through great personal struggle and strain, I grew ten inches during the next two years. However, I was still always a step behind, not quite good enough for the school teams but much more interested in sports than academics.

I was, however, accomplished enough to make the college JV basketball team as an ardent bench warmer. Warming the bench is an important role on any team ... even the JV team of a small Christian college needed a few spare bodies giving some semblance of a team. This vital function was performed by my good friend Dan and I… sitting on the end of the bench, backslapping, opponent mocking, anything for the team. It was not particularly glamorous but was a legitimate alternative to serious study, and I think free socks were part of the deal. I was still never quite good enough for varsity level.

Upon graduation, I noticed the balance began to shift. As time went on my varsity friends started to plump up and slow down. The differential was narrowing. By the time I was in my early to middle twenties I could more than keep up. My fifteen minutes of fame came in the far north of Saskatchewan, Canada when I was the leading scorer of the Northern Saskatchewan Men's Basketball League. It was great to discover that without skates, hockey players play very poor defense.

Over the years, I considered myself at least a semi-athlete, which means I could normally keep up with the overweight slow guys in the gym. Playing sports well into my forties, I planned to be running with the kids when I was sixty. Suddenly, however, the large, slow people were getting older and quicker, and I was getting older and slower. Seeing fifty pounds of overweight former athlete roll on by was more than a bit disconcerting.

There were other changes. As the pastor of a busy church, I found my stamina severely affected. My planning and organization seemed to be less and less effective. Routine tasks took twice as long. My handwriting was getting worse and worse. Knowing that a sloppy signature indicated an advanced level of education, I was pleased that I could pass as well educated by signature alone. Friends and family started to nag... why are you limping... why don't you swing your arm when you walk... is your arm hurt... why are you shuffling your feet?

One day I went to pick up a dish and was unable to do so. The previous Sunday I had fallen at church bruising myself badly. It looked like something needed attention. I went to the doctor who ordered an MRI. They took all kinds of pictures of my brain... perfectly normal they said. It was good to have confirmation... my kids have never been too sure. The next step was a visit to the neurologist who went through the basic neurological movement type diagnostics and informed me matter-of-factly that I had early Parkinson's disease.

Quickly analyzing the situation, it struck me that early Parkinson's disease is a lot like... just like... real Parkinson's disease. All kinds of words came to my mind... debilitating... devastating... discouraging... and probably some more d words which would remain verbally unexpressed. He gave me a prescription and said to come back in a few months.

What does a neurologist in Poughkeepsie, New York know after all? I am one hour away from one of the top movement disorder centers in the country, Columbia Presbyterian Hospital in Manhattan. We set an appointment, and believe it or not, they did the same diagnostics and came to the same conclusion except they didn't call it early Parkinson's disease. They called it Parkinson's disease (PD).

Parkinson's is a disease of the brain. A definitive cause has not been identified, although evidence points toward a combination of genetic pre-disposition and exposure to some environmental toxin. Whatever the cause, the brain cells which produce dopamine begin to die off. Dopamine is a neurotransmitter which enables the messages to travel from the brain to the various parts of the body. By the time a Parkinson's patient shows any symptoms, 80% of these dopamine producing cells have died off. From that point on, the disease only gets worse. There is no cure. The most common symptom is tremor... usually starting on one side... often in the hand and then progressing to the rest of the body. 15 to 20% of Parkinson's patients never get tremor. Other symptoms of Parkinson's disease are stiffness, slowness of movement, confusion, memory loss, instability leading to falls, aches and pains, and difficulty writing. Any function of the body can be affected. Breathing, swallowing, digestion, bladder control ... all can be affected or slowed down by Parkinson's disease.

Driving home from the neurologist, I was shaking my head. These are the kinds of things that happen to other people. Over the years I've preached that instead of asking *why me* when the trials come, the question is why *not* me? Would I be able to practice what I preached? I wasn't too sure.

I had a plan for my retirement years. I was going to work really hard, so I could retire at sixty-five, settle into a church with a small salary/stipend, and spend my time doing all the things I loved to do as a pastor. The tough assignments would fall to the young senior pastor. Some days, I couldn't wait for those golden years. That was my plan. Suddenly the horizon had changed. With kids in college, no house to live in, no job, growing uncertainty, the plan had changed.

If you watch (not stare at) people with Parkinson's disease the tremor is very often obvious. Especially in times of stress, the hands can shake uncontrollably in a "marble-rolling" kind of motion. We PD people hold our hands down or keep them in our pockets so others will not notice. As the disease progresses the entire body can be affected by the spasms. At this point in time, ten years following my diagnosis, friends at church have learned to keep their distance during coffee hour. Random movement has smacked more than one cup of coffee from the hands of an innocent bystander. The tremor of PD is very obvious, but there are those crises, less obvious visually, that shake our lives just as profoundly.

What do you do when life shakes you up? How do you live when the plan changes? There are all kinds of coping mechanisms both negative and positive. But denial, false hope, busyness, blame, anger, and bitterness tend to be the responses of least resistance. How do you respond to facing an incurable diagnosis?

<u>Battle Plan from the General</u>

The Bible is full of examples of people who face the unexpected realities of life with faith and courage. Joshua was one of these people. Joshua was a great military leader who led the people of Israel into the promised land of Canaan. His example can be a help and inspiration to us. In his response to the unexpected, we can find a "battle plan from the general" if you will.

I will reference the Old Testament passage of Joshua 1:1-9 throughout the book. Let me summarize the story. Moses obviously was a great hero of Israeli history. He had delivered his people from the bondage of Egypt and had brought them to the brink of entering the promised land. Along the way, Joshua had been his loyal military leader. But now God had a new plan for Joshua: "After the death of Moses the servant of the Lord, the Lord said to Joshua son of Nun, Moses' aide: 'Moses my servant is dead. Now then, you and all these people, get ready to cross the Jordan River into the land I am about to give to them, to the Israelites.'" (*Joshua 1:1*)

Joshua suddenly found himself as the divinely appointed designated heroic leader of the chosen people of God. Being the Prime Minister of Israel was not Joshua's plan. He was a soldier, not a politician. He was a fighter, not a talker. How would he respond?

There are lessons we can learn from Joshua that are helpful as we face those things that shake us up in life. *How do you respond when life shakes you up?*

FACE THE FACTS

ACCEPT THE FEELINGS

COUNT THE BLESSINGS

LIVE THE FAITH

TRUST THE FUTURE TO GOD

These five points are not presented as a linear step-by-step procedure. They are not steps as much as aspects of dealing with the hurt of life. I needed to come back again and again to face the facts that I had Parkinson's disease, and I needed to decide to face the reality of the whole thing. I still get afraid for the future and need to decide to trust my future to a loving, personal God. These five aspects are "faith options;" decisions to be made in times that are overwhelming and stressful. My goal is to present, not a process, but perhaps a play book, giving options with which we can respond by faith.

1

FACE THE FACTS

"Moses my servant is dead..."

Get Your Flu Shot

It saddens me to admit that I received my first flu shot this year. There are certain groups of people who need flu shots more than others and are strongly encouraged to do so. I have never been a part of this group, but having just turned sixty, dealing with a chronic disease, with a wife in public nursing, I qualify on all counts. There are several factors conspiring together that influenced me toward this decision. One of these factors was living with a loving/nagging medical practitioner. The fearful warning, prevalent at the time, of the coming global epidemic of swine flu was another. The clincher was my reading of the book by John M. Barry, *The Great Influenza Epidemic of 1918,* which is a fascinating and harrowing account the incredible death toll of that terrible epidemic.

In the winter of 1918, the coldest the American Midwest had ever endured, history's most lethal strain of the influenza virus was born. Over the next year, the global fatality count was between 50 and 100 million. During the two years that this scourge ravaged the earth, a fifth of the world's population was infected. The flu was most deadly for people ages twenty to forty and infected 28% of all Americans.

An estimated 675,000 Americans died of influenza during the pandemic, ten times as many as in the recent world war. Of all the U.S. soldiers who died in Europe, half of them fell to the influenza virus, not the enemy. Over 43,000 of the servicemen mobilized for WWI died of influenza.

On September 7, 1917, Fort Devens, a military camp thirty-five miles northwest of Boston, saw the first case of flu. Within two weeks 20% of the recruits were infected. A hospital equipped for 1,200 was bursting with 6,000 patients. The doctors and nurses were dying as quickly as the patients. Dr. Roy Gist wrote that men would report to the hospital and:

> Two hours after admission they have mahogany spots over the cheek bones, and a few hours later you can begin to see the Cyanosis extending from their ears and spreading all over the face, until it is hard to distinguish the colored men from the white. Within hours death is final after excruciating pain, with bleeding from the nose, ears and even eyes. (*The Great Influenza Epidemic of 1918*)

The first case in Philadelphia, a city of 1.75 million, was reported on October 1, 1918. Within ten days hundreds of thousands were infected with hundreds dying each day. Bodies were stacked like cord wood waiting for the death wagons to pick them up. In New York City alone 21,000 became orphans and twice that many lost one parent.

In the midst of this real to life horror movie, the government forbade the newspapers from publishing anything but positive, encouraging news about the pandemic. In order to dispel the national alarm caused by "exaggerated reports," the Associated Press reported, "…while there are about 4,500 cases (at Great Lakes Training Station) the situation in general is much improved." Hundreds of newspapers continued the national message propagated by the Surgeon General: "there is no cause for alarm if precautions are followed" and "the epidemic is on the wane." Colonel Philip Jones told the Associated Press, "The so called Spanish influenza is nothing more or less than old fashioned grippe." "Don't Get Scared" was the advice printed in virtually every newspaper. Almost daily it repeated, "Don't Let Flu Frighten you to Death" and "Don't Panic." As a result, thousands more died as bodies piled on the streets and front porches of our great cities.

50 to 100 million deaths is bad news. The only hope for survival was to face the reality and take desperate action searching for a vaccine. Fortunately great scientists such as William Welch, William Gorgas, and Simon Flexner toiled tirelessly to develop

vaccines that were at least partially effective. They faced the facts, which were overwhelming in their scope. Facing the facts did not stop the horror; the bodies still piled up in the streets, and the hospitals still flowed with blood. But the recovery was impossible until they recognized the enemy.

Hopefully none of us will ever need to face the devastation of a worldwide pandemic, but when life is unfair, when you are mistreated, abandoned, laid off, arrested – whatever the crisis – the decision of faith is to face the facts. We can face the realities of life, but not on our own, only with the help, strength, and guidance of a loving, personal God.

Battle Plan from the General

Joshua had some devastating, life and death realities to face as well. God speaks to Joshua, and he doesn't pull any punches. Moses is *dead*…talk about blunt. We don't like the bad news. Maybe you have noticed - bad news does not send an engraved invitation. Bad news comes suddenly - unexpectedly. When life shakes you up, it slaps you in the face, and it's the last thing you expect.

God speaks to Joshua. Moses is dead - now it's your turn to lead. Think about it. Moses was one of the big guys. God had spoken to Moses in person on the top of Mount Sinai. Joshua had watched as Moses hand delivered the Ten Commandments, still smoking from the hand of God. He had watched Moses deal with all the annoying, whining, grumbling people as he led them heroically across the Sinai desert. He watched Moses stretch his rod out and part the Red Sea. It was Cecil B. Demille, in *real* Technicolor and real life. Joshua had big shoes, or rather sandals, to fill. Joshua was in over his head.

Personal

We don't like the news that shatters our plans and dashes our dreams. I did not like hearing I had an incurable disease. Immediately, I wanted a second opinion. There must be some mistake. Shortly after diagnosis, I was gathering information, searching online, educating myself on what I was facing. I received a large manila envelope from one of the PD research/support groups. It was stuffed full of more information than I ever wanted or needed.

The first thing to fall out of the envelope was a royal blue business sized card with bright yellow letters – with the words *I AM NOT RETARDED* emblazoned on the front. The back explained that the carrier of the card was not retarded but rather had Parkinson's disease. I could use this card to let people know that I may have trouble with my words, but to be patient because it would just take me longer. So the good news was that I was *not* retarded - the not so good news is I just looked and acted retarded. I had to face it. I had an incurable disease. I didn't like it ...I don't like it ... it was not ... is not good news.

5

There were frightening financial realities to face. We had a plan for getting the kids through college and preparing for retirement. Over the years, my wife Brenda has worked as a home care nurse caring especially for pediatric cases. She is amazingly gifted as a care giver and considers it a ministry. She loves "her children" as her own. The plan was that as soon as our nest was empty, or maybe even during the last few high school years, we would begin to work on our nest egg. I would continue as a full time pastor, and my wife would work full time as a nurse. This would help the kids through school and help us invest in retirement so we could buy a house and settle in . . . hopefully near family and grandchildren.

The problem was that God did not check in with my broker. Possibly because he knew I didn't have a broker. Being omniscient and all he probably also knew of my almost-would-be broker who after meeting with me offered the gentle reminder that investment required capital funds. In other words, "people with no money have no need for my services." I had no input in the matter and received no notice of the unwelcome nemesis. It made no sense to me or anyone else I knew.

Our plan was clearly a good plan. It was almost like God didn't get it. After all, we had "sacrificed" to live in a church owned parsonage our whole life. (I wish I could write another book about the blessings of raising kids in a parsonage ... yes you heard me right!) Hadn't we given over and above the tithe of our income to God's work in the church, missions, and various building projects and special needs? We deserved at least a say in the deal.

Lest you think that "facing the facts" is a formula for feeling groovy in five easy steps, when life turns bad … this was certainly not my experience. Facing the facts, the hard realities of life, *is* a onetime decision but also an arduous never ending process.

Michael J. Fox's book, *Lucky Man: The Diary of an Incurable Optimist* has been an invaluable help in writing this book. Upon being diagnosed with PD, the neurologist told him he had at least ten good years of production before he would need to step back and retire. I was forty-nine years old and kind of accepted the ten more years of production scenario, in an *"I'll deal with all that ten years from now"* sort of way. I was not about to consider that in two years, the lay leadership would be doing most of my work in the church and that in four years I would be on disability.

In retrospect, I had been slowing down for a number of years. Weekly sermons, which typically involved six to eight hours of preparation, now took twelve to twenty hours. Our church was blessed with twelve lay pastors (very apostolic I thought) who provided practical care within the congregation. Meetings would normally be held every six weeks. These meetings were now happening perhaps twice a year. For many years, I had prepared a daily devotional follow up to the weekly sermon, hoping that if my people had no idea what I was saying, maybe it would make more sense in print. Somehow I just didn't seem to be able to continue that on a weekly basis. There were times I was plagued with guilt because I was just too exhausted to visit a parishioner in the hospital. I needed to face up to the reality that I needed help.

Letting go of that which I loved so much ... allowing others to fill in and make up for my deficiency was heart wrenching. So many people were so responsive to the ministry needs of the church. The church where I served as pastor for fourteen years was planning a $1,000,000 expansion. During the two years before my retirement, the building committee met without me. Nominations, elections, finances, Christian education ... most of the functions of the church were cared for by volunteers with my two secretaries basically acting as a pastor in planning and facilitating the activities of the church. Sunday mornings, I would preach in the early service, sleep during Sunday School, then preach once more in the 11 am service. There were times when I asked our youth/associate pastor, to take over in the middle of the service while I took a seven minute nap before preaching. Pastoral ministry became more and more difficult.

My effectiveness as a pastor and leader was clearly diminished. I didn't like it. This was clear in a journal entry late one night:

May 15, 2002

I don't want to be like this the rest of my life.   I don't want my wife to have to live with this stinking blank stare spaced out look.   I don't want people calling the house wondering if I'm able to answer the phone. I want to visit all day Saturday.   I want to go early to church, talk to people who come early, preach two services and talk to some more people.   I want to be part of realizing that we messed up the building program and there's a much better way to do it.

I don't want to keep telling people that I am too impaired to do their weddings, baptisms, and if they die they need to make other arrangements.   I want to keep harassing with District licensed ministers on the Credentials Board.   I'm not sure if I like seeing them squirm or am deeply concerned about the leadership of the church; probably both. I want to stay out late with some with nutty people without feeling that I will be a wreck on Sunday because of it.   I am so tired of stupid voice software (that) won't work.   I don't want to be someone different ... I want to be myself.   It is that too much to ask?

No

9

PD significantly impairs the function of the frontal lobe of the brain. This area of the brain has an administrative function, prioritizing and filtering out that which is unimportant. Parkinsonian people tend to be overwhelmed and unable to focus in an ADD kind of way.

June 20, 2003 (Sitting in my office at the church)

This is what happens when my mind goes hyper. My mind has just jumped in the last one or two minutes from going to Sam's, going to the bank, going to the driving range, going fishing, going to the wake, talking to Louise, working on Colossians, working on the cycle of victorious living diagram, meeting with Gary, going swimming, working out, taking the digital recorder back, fixing supper. What do I do to short-circuit my head from this mind blitz?

This is not like me. It is why I feel lonely or mixed up sometimes. I keep missing myself... but I am really still there. When I'm writing ... that's the real me. When I'm goofing off ... that's the real me. When I cried... I guess that was the real me... just didn't know it. When I preach... it's not a persona... it's the real me (but God's words). So when I miss myself I just need to remember I'm still there... for the most part I'm still pretty visible. When I am trying to help people... it's the real me... but only when I'm not trying to fix the whole world. When I am walking in puddles with Andrew... there I am... and I think it is a real Andrew as well. When hugging my wife, marveling at Jonathan's talent or admiring Christina as a gift from God ... I am most myself. When I ask for help from friends... sometimes too often... I hope it's the real me, not manipulating, not overly dependent... hoping to be a help to them as well.

Anyway this whole weird situation is interesting, exciting, hopeful, terrible, strange and the working of God continues in and through the whole thing.

Many who read this book will have stories of parental abuse as a child, the lingering pain as an adult victim of divorce, teachers who are not fair, an employer who has thrown them away like a used rag, friends who destroyed their reputation, a pastor who betrayed their confidence, a diagnosis that is overwhelming. None of this is good news. The fact remains ... and I seldom if ever use this word but ... **duh** ... bad news, by definition, is bad.

Why?

The natural response when bad news bullies its way into our lives is – WHY? This instinctive reaction to crisis brings doubts and fears, and we wonder: "Where is God?" "Why is he doing this to me?" "What have I done wrong?" Tragically there are many whose faith is shattered in the disillusionment and despair of unanswered questions. God is viewed as capricious - even cruel.

We so much want things to make sense. It is so much easier to endure pain and suffering if there is a reason for it. As people of faith, we try to make sense of it all.

- God's got everything under control.
- God is just trying to teach you something.
- God will not give you more than you can handle.
- This is a test that will make you stronger.
- This too shall pass.
- I've got to believe that everything happens; happens for a reason.

Each of these statements is true to one degree or another. God does teach us in the midst of the trying times of life. We do have the promise in Scripture that God will not send us more than we are able to handle. First Corinthians 10:13 says that God: "... will not let you be tempted beyond what you can bear. But when you are tempted, he will also provide a way out so that you can stand up under it." The Scripture also teaches us that God does work in our lives to build perseverance, strength, and faith: "Consider it pure joy, my brothers, whenever you face trials of many kinds, because you know that the testing of your faith develops perseverance. Perseverance must finish its work so that you may be mature and complete, not lacking anything." (*James 1:6-7*) We say that "this too shall pass." But what about the times when the pain, suffering, injustice or abuse does not pass? It just stays. The assertion that everything happens for a reason brings little if any comfort. Instead we face even more questions and doubts. If we Christians believe in an all-powerful and personal God and we do, is all our suffering part of God's plan? Is "everything" God's will? Why would God's plan include that which is insufferable and seemingly so meaningless? Did God send me my disease? I can see all kinds of ways that God's grace has taught me, strengthened me, and opened up opportunities for ministry that I would not otherwise have known. If he did, however, send this disease, I wish he had sent it registered mail. I would not have signed for the delivery.

Then where do we go? Does God ordain that I leave the door open so that I stub my toe... to teach me patience? A God who is responsible for all that happens becomes the author or at least the co-conspirator of all that is evil as well as all that is good. Is God really in control of everything in the world? Is God really in control when one of our children rebels, turns from God, and rejects the love of family? Is his or her destructive decision and the resulting devastation, pain and loss God's will? How can God be fully in control if he wills that people do not do his will? WHY? The questions haunt us. So often it makes no sense to us.

Harold S Kushner, in his book *When Bad Things Happen to Good People*, asked the question: "... but why do we have to insist on everything being reasonable? Why must everything happen for a specific reason? Why can't we let the universe have a few rough edges?" He comes to the conclusion that God is in fact not all-powerful; that there are those things that he *cannot* control. Kushner concludes that we should never pray for healing, convenience, or fortune. We should rather pray for God's strength, peace, wisdom, and help. He sees a God who does not interfere with the random laws of nature, or the consequences of evil decisions, or the natural occurrence of disease. It is difficult to reconcile, however, a God of limited power with the revelation of scripture. Many Christians, myself included, see an all-powerful God who loves us so much that he has chosen to limit his power; giving us the choice to love him or reject him.

There is much I would recommend in the book *When Bad Things Happen to Good People*. As we struggle to find some sense or reason in the struggles and stresses of life, this is a good resource. As Christians, however, we believe in a God who *does* intervene. Why does God intervene in one specific time and place but not another? All of these things are more than perplexing. We want God to be in control. We want there to be a reason for everything that happens. But where God's providence begins and ends is often difficult to ascertain. How often does God overrule the effects of the laws of nature or save us from the consequences of our personal decisions or the decisions of others?

I'm afraid that any definitive answer to all these questions is beyond my expertise. All of my in depth reflection upon infinity/eternity/providence brings me face to face with the reality that life unavoidably comes with a hearty dose of mystery. My purpose in sharing my faith journey is to encourage and challenge people of faith to respond with hope and confidence to crises in their lives. The good news of the gospel tells us that an all-powerful and personal God desires to live in a loving relationship with his creation.

Face the Facts… life comes unavoidably

with a hearty dose of mystery.

Denial

The first response when life shakes you up – Face the Facts. Don't deny reality. Denial is not a response of faith. Faith is not wishful thinking but rather a foundation upon which you can base your response to the crises of life. In no way is Christian faith some sort of spiritualized denial mechanism. You might rightfully say that faith is a crutch, for we do indeed lean hard on the love of God and the care of his people. We do need to stand upon that which is solid and dependable. But again, faith does not entail pretending that the crisis does not exist.

Take Bill for example. Bill was always fantastic. He was retired and well into his senior years, but he was one upbeat guy. Every week I would ask Bill how he was doing. The response was always "fantastic." One Sunday, after being away a couple weeks, I didn't see Bill and asked if he was okay … "Oh hadn't you heard - Bill is dead." Apparently he had terminal cancer and you'll have to excuse me for raining on his parade, but I am thinking that dying of cancer is something different than fantastic. Faith is not denial. Denial tends to be subconscious, an involuntary response. The premise of this book is that the response to crises can be on purpose rather than involuntary.

Denial is not always harmful. There are times that denial is necessary as a first step in coping with unthinkably bad news. As a sophomore in high school, my son Ryan had been having headaches and dizzy spells at school. We took him to the doctor who immediately ordered an MRI. It was on a Friday afternoon that my wife walked through the back door of our church parsonage with an MRI film. She was white as a sheet and nearly paralyzed with fear. The MRI revealed a large white mass the size of a softball on the right frontal lobe of his brain.

We were frightened. We knew it was serious. But in spite of what we "knew" … he still went to the New York Mets game that afternoon at Shea Stadium. How stupid could we be? The facts were so overwhelming that we were unable to act as though we believed it. The doctor called after hours and suggested Ryan should go to the emergency room. Joyce, a church member and good friend volunteered to brave the New York traffic; driving to Queens to bring him home early. When Ryan returned from the Mets game, we took him to the emergency room and after waiting five hours the neurologist on call said he was busy and would see him in five days. More denial. I had been diagnosed with PD a few months earlier, there was conflict and criticism in the church concerning a building project, we were feeling the pressure, and we just could not assimilate a brain tumor on top of everything else. Ryan even went to school on Monday morning.

The good news is that I took the MRI to Columbia Presbyterian Hospital and my neurologists in the Movement Disorder Center dropped everything to call Sloane Kettering Hospital for Cancer Treatment on the other side of Manhattan. Making like a New York cab driver I madly transported the MRI across town. The surgeon insisted that we "get him down here immediately." By that afternoon my son was in intensive care at Cornell-Weir Hospital for Special Surgery. On Thursday, Dr. Souweidane, a world class pediatric surgeon performed the operation. I will never forget the feelings of fear, dread, and hope as my son was taken away from us and rolled through the doors … understanding that anything could happen and knowing that the news is not always good.

The tumor was fully removed, uninvolved with the brain, and totally benign with no trace of cancer. We are so thankful for the doctors, surgeons and staff of these amazing medical centers. Ryan missed his last two years of high school basketball, but was able to play two years of college ball. It was a gift from God, and he is now a social worker in Boston with plans for seminary in the near future.

The first natural response to trauma is denial. In an interesting way, it is the first step in facing the facts. It is that time in which the facts are "known" but we act as though they are not real. In this sense, *initial denial* is a helpful tool as a step toward facing reality.

Denial becomes a negative response when it continues beyond the initial state of shock. There is a type of pseudo-Christian response which ignores the seriousness of bad news and tragic circumstances. The attitude is that God is still on the throne and everything will work out for the best. Later I will introduce you to an important tenet of the faith, "*Cheer Up ... someday you're gonna die.*" By faith we believe in eternal life. The reality of heaven does not, however, guarantee that I will be healed of my disease in this life. Jesus does not teach that the life of a disciple is a life without suffering, pain, disease, and persecution. Living by faith is not denying the suffering but rather living out the life of hope and faith even if the suffering is not miraculously removed.

Any denial of the difficult realities of life is a denial of

the adequacy of Christ, in whom we place our faith.

Jesus is the cornerstone of our faith. He did not come to live among us, so that we could escape real life. He came, calling us as His followers, to get all wrapped up in realities of a world full of sin, oppression, and injustice... seeking to save those who are lost.

When you lose your job... face the facts. When you are stricken with illness don't act as though it doesn't exist. When you fail... fess up... face the music... suffer the embarrassment. When you sin, don't pretend it's a mistake, confess the sin. There's no way to deal with the things that shake your life until you look them straight in the eye. (Pink slips, diagnoses, rejection, and other trials certainly must have eyes ... they find us so readily).

There are other less than positive responses to the trials of life.

Complaint

It was a father/son moment. I had picked Dave up from school, and we went to enjoy pizza inter-dispersed with the normal parental prying session. Why do parents have to get so personal? Anyway, we ordered our pizza, waited as patiently as possible for a lively junior higher and a busy pastor. (Neither one of us waits well.) We kept looking toward the kitchen door with anticipation.

The pizza finally arrived, and after saying a very few brief words of thanks, I suspended my prying and we dug in. If anticipation is half of the enjoyment ... we were missing half the fun. The pizza was cold with barely a brushing of tomato sauce and just a little bit too tough for my fifty year old teeth. Being in an assertive mood, I called the waiter over and pointed out the injustice of having trusted such a fine institution to provide a quality product and to receive instead that which was so far below reasonable expectations. The waiter was all apologies and quickly returned to the kitchen. Ten minutes later we received our pizza, hot and steaming, with too MUCH sauce. Topping it all off, the waiter said, "The manager says the pizza is free today."

It was a very cool deal for my son to see me at my courageous best. I stood up for my rights, and that poor waiter never had a chance. My son was seriously impressed about the free pizza we enjoyed. Not long after we were in a restaurant with the family. It hadn't been five minutes after receiving our meals that Dave followed my stalwart example saying, "This spaghetti is terrible. Tell the waitress we want free spaghetti."

We live in a complaining society. We deserve a break today. We deserve to be treated well. If we are inconvenienced, ignored, or even if fate deals us a bad hand, someone needs to hear about it. When life shakes you up, the "path of least resistance" is complaint. If we take an objective step back and consider the value of complaint, there is little benefit.

Henri Nouwen, in *The Return of the Prodigal Son*, had an insightful perspective on the nature of complaint:

> One thing I am sure. Complaining is self-perpetuating and counterproductive. Whenever I express my complaints in the hope of evoking pity and receiving the satisfaction I so much desire, the result is always the opposite of what I tried to get. A complainer is hard to live with, and very few people know how to respond to the complaints made by a self-rejecting person. The tragedy is that often, the complaint, once expressed, leads to that which is most feared: further rejection.

I may still send my cold pizza back, but the salient point is that complaint is not a response of faith and maturity. Complaint is wishful petulant thinking … wishing in a self- focused way that I should never have to face the pain, trials, and loss of living in a world where pain, disease, ignorance, and sin are a reality. Chapter Four will focus on the faith decision to *"Live the Faith,"* as an alternative to complaint, escape, blame etc. but for now … the focus is upon complaint as a negative response, rather than **Facing the Facts.**

Self-Pity

Another memory (let me know if you are getting tired of my family stories.) One morning I received a call from my daughter's elementary school. Christina, in 5th grade at the time, was apparently hurt in the playground and the nurse was asking me to come and get her. Being busy in the office, I said I could get there in half an hour or so, to which the nurse responded, "You need to come right now!" Of course I left right away, still having no details of the problem.

Apparently a three inch tree branch had tipped into the playground where the kids were pulling it back, sitting on it, and going for a ride upon its release. Christina was waiting her turn when another child pulled the branch back while she was in front of it. The branch was released sending my daughter on a completely unexpected, very painful and frightening ride. The branch caught her in the mouth, splitting her lip, driving her front two teeth into her mouth, and tearing the palate. It was a sight no parent should ever have to see.

We rushed her to an oral surgeon with a gruff, insensitive bedside or rather dentist-chair-side manner, which was more than annoying. I held her hand as he pulled the teeth forward, pushed them in place, and stitched up the palate all the while telling my ten year old not to cry because it wasn't his fault she was injured. He was a grouchy old guy, which was the bad news ... his being a good surgeon was the good news. We picked up pain medication and went home to wait on her hand and foot and help her recover the best we could.

Just about this time, one of my sons came home, and threw down his back pack, saying, "This was the worst day of my life!" He began to tell his sad story of forgotten homework or unfair teachers or whatever was the crisis of the day; he was looking for some sympathy for the angst of his day when he suddenly saw his sister. Her face was swollen and bruised; she was obviously being pampered within an inch of her life ... his countenance fell. Clearly his sister had sucked every ounce of available pity from the hearts of his family. Seeing there was no pity left to be had, he left his back pack and trudged wearily up to his room. It seemed like he was the only invitee to his pity party that day.

What is it about a pity party that we enjoy so much? Pity, like complaint is another "path of least resistance" response to crises. Pity is the opposite of compassion. Compassion says, "I feel your pain; how can I help?" Pity says, "I feel *my* pain; how can you help *me*?" Self-pity is an open invitation to a party that no one really wants to attend but is unable to refuse. The RSVP is not an option; it is not received in the mail but rather delivered in person.

Again, like complaint, pity is not a response of faith. Faith is facing the facts, part of which is the living through pain, inconvenience, injustice, or sorrow that accompany the crises of life. Self-pity turns us inward as a negative, escapist, reactionary response to the insecurities of life. A faith response is pro-active, standing strong:

> Stand firm then, with the belt of truth buckled around your waist, with the breastplate of righteousness in place, and with your feet fitted with the readiness that comes from the gospel of peace. In addition to all this, take up the shield of faith, with which you can extinguish all the flaming arrows of the evil one. Take the helmet of salvation and the sword of the Spirit, which is the word of God. *(Ephesians 6:14-17)*

As followers of Jesus Christ, we are not without resources. Pain and crisis do not change the truth upon which we stand. The good news of the gospel is an ever present reality. The shield of a practical and personal faith remains as a protection against the attack of negativity and temptation. We are protected by the helmet of salvation so that when we are shaken by life we can respond on purpose in a pro-active way. We will look further at some of these issues when we discuss, Living Your Faith, as a purposeful practical life style decision. But for now: ***Tear up the invitation!***

Panic

Another common and less than positive response is panic. As an eight to ten year old, growing up in a town just outside of Boston, I was part of a gang of boys. This was gang activity in the best sense of the word. These were the unenlightened days of the late 50's so it was politically correct to play cops and robbers, cowboys and Indians, knights of the round table, and AFL football (back in the days before New England Patriots), but the thing we loved most was "raiding the girls." The girls would be playing house or whatever other girly thing they happened to be doing, and we would swoop in as marauding bandits, over turn their tea set, frighten their dolls, and generally wreak havoc and misery upon their existence.

One day, during a particularly successful raid, we turned to see Mr. Lebrun. He was on a mission to defend the honor of his little girl. From our perspective he was big, ugly, scary and very mad ... steam from his ears ... froth from his mouth ... coming to save the girls and demolish the enemy. Clearly it was fight or flight time, and knowing that fight was not an option, I burst into all out flight mode. I began to run ... and lo and behold he started chasing me. Did he not know my older brother was the ring leader of this nefarious plot?

I put my head down, ducked into a neighboring nursery and began running through the trees. He was getting closer. I could feel his hot breath on my neck. He was just about to get me when I found myself with my legs spinning in midair, not unlike Wiley Coyote in the Road Runner cartoon. I had run straight off the precipice of a sheer cliff and was sure I would fall to my death. I found myself flat on my back after a frightening fall of at least four feet.

When things get tough the easiest thing to do is panic ... worry ourselves sick ... do something stupid ... take things in our own hands ... run off a cliff in fear. We don't need to panic. We are not alone as our God is an ever present help in time of trouble. We are not alone as the family of God is a help and support. A loving God sends his Spirit to comfort, strengthen, and lead. We have a guide in the words of God and as we listen and seek the wisdom of an infinite God, he will show us the next step to take when life shakes you up. I am quite sure the next step taken in obedient response to the words of God will not be off a cliff.

Our place of greatest fear and danger is most

often the place of greatest blessing.

Bitterness

For the purposes of this book, I am defining anger as an unavoidable human response on the feeling level. We will look at the feelings of anger in the next chapter. But here we will look at bitterness as a *choice.*

My family and I are blessed with a beautiful back yard, a one-third acre lot with half of that covered with trees and flowers around a small in-ground pool that is used every day during the summer. There were two trees in our back yard that apart from exhaling oxygen back into the atmosphere were of very little use. These trees crowded out the growth of the flowers, blocked the sunlight from the pool, and in the fall, shed bushels of leaves to fill the pool and yard. I even think I heard those naked trees snickering as I raked the yard and dredged their leafy remnants out of the pool.

My wife is wiser than I and suggested we cut the trees down. It hardly seemed right environmentally, but the more we thought about it the more it made sense. We cut down three trees, the two leaf factories and an evergreen that was growing too close to the house for safety. This summer was the first without the trees. The flowers look better and healthier than ever, the pool was 10-15 degrees warmer, and I am currently looking out my back window in November having spent a total of ninety minutes raking leaves this fall.

We enjoyed the flowers, the sunlight and the warmth this summer, but we noticed that those trees began to grow back. It was clear that in a few years they would be blocking the sun and crowding out the flowers again. In response to their stubbornness, we treated those tree stumps with defoliant. We did not want to nurture the growth of those trees blocking the light. They were an unwelcome presence in our yard.

Why would anyone invite that which is unwelcome and negative into their lives? Why would anyone cultivate and nurture anger? What is it that draws us to the perverse torture/pleasure of reliving and remembering the pain and injustice of life? Anger is a very real, powerful, and even healthy response to the inequities and iniquities of life. The feelings of anger, however, are like emotional stem cells.

(I will refrain from the ethical controversy surrounding stem cells as related to neurological disease, just to mention that stem cells are cells in the early developmental stages that through the miraculous creative power of God (or mother nature, or the amazing creative force of zillions of years and blind chance ... but I digress) these cells have the ability to morph into all the various cells that become a human body.)

Feelings of anger can morph into bitterness and a self-absorbed perspective that strangles the sense of hope and joy in life. Feelings of anger — as emotional/spiritual stem cells in the petri dish of the human heart, soaking in self-centeredness and revenge— yield a rancor that is hard, cold, and faithless. This bitterness can consume every waking moment, poison every relationship, and skew every decision.

On the other hand, these same feelings in the petri dish of the same human heart saturated with grace, faith and forgiveness yield a gentle spirit and a compassionate heart. Henri Nouwen speaks of the wounded healer, reminding us that it is those who have been hurt most deeply that can care with the greatest compassion. And as Jesus explained to his disciples, as Mary Magdalene anointed his feet, he who has been forgiven much, loves much.

We will look more closely at the grace-full way that God's grace turns pain and sorrow into compassion in subsequent chapters but for now, face the facts with an acceptance that does not cultivate anger into the cold angst of bitterness.

Blame

Blame is closely related to bitterness. Blame is the perverse all-consuming need to attach a name, personality, institution or deity to the cultivated anger which *is* bitterness. We have asked the question, "Why would we ever cultivate feelings of anger when they produce such bitterness?" In the same way we can ask the question, "Why would we ever focus so much on establishing blame when it produces an ever deepening bitterness?"

In blame, negative and/or hostile motives are assigned to the blamee, whoever or whatever that may be. In a self-absorbed way, we foster a sense of the idea that, "my life and happiness are

28

important" and he, she, they, God, (fill in the blank) have no right to disturb that. Can you see a pattern developing where a faith-less response turns us inward and away from the resources of God and toward the poverty of self-sufficiency? Whereas, a faith response turns us away from the sink hole of self-focus and toward the love, grace, and strength of God himself.

(Did I mention to let me know when you are tired of my personal stories?) My son Jonathan was in Nairobi, Kenya for six months of volunteer service. He was teaching at the African Nazarene University, consulting with student government leaders and helping in any way he could. One morning, we got a disturbing message, *"Hey Mom I am very sick. I don't know what it is, but it's bad."* That was not what you want to hear from a son on the other side of the world. He had fever, aching, nausea, loss of appetite and was expelling remnants of human ingestion from all directions. Our biggest fears were malaria which would be with him for the rest of his life and typhoid fever which could be four - six weeks of high fever, pain, and weakness. The good news was that it was neither of these diseases. The bad news was that he had an amoeba.

I googled amoeba disease and the first headline I saw was the following...

"6 die from brain-eating amoeba after swimming"

It sounds like science fiction but it's true: A killer amoeba living in lakes enters the body through the nose and attacks the **brain** where it feeds until the person is dead. (Associated Press as reported on www.msnbc.msn.com, 9/28/2007.) These amoebae are one cell protozoa that are ingested in the drinking water, especially in developing countries. They set up homestead in the digestive system for an incubation period and then reproduce and make their way to the liver, pancreas, kidney and brain. Fortunately, the amoebae in question were of the less virulent strain and routinely treated with amoebacide medication. If these invasive parasites were not eliminated they would have multiplied and affected the whole body.

Bitterness is an invasive parasite that will reproduce and infect every area of life. By establishing blame, we setup a target upon which to direct our anger. The result is an environment for the unwelcome invader of bitterness to multiply and intensify. We do not face the facts, rather we spend our time and energy blaming rather than responding in faith. Purposely turning away from the blame game and turning toward a faith response is a necessary step in facing the realities of life with grace, strength, and resolve.

Henri Nouwen, speaks of the freedom and deliverance from the shackles of blame and bitterness:

> Imagine your having no need at all to judge anybody.
> Imagine your having no desire to decide someone is a
> good or bad person. Imagine your being completely free
> from the feeling that you have to make up your mind about

the morality of someone's behavior. Imagine that you could say: I am judging no one!

(*Here and Now*)

Not one of us is exempt from the shattering assault of the tragic and unjust events of life. People do not always smile at you. Good fortune does not always fill your life with sunlight. There are times when the darkness of pain, trials, suffering and injustice consume your existence. Facing the facts, living by faith involves an acceptance of the trials and suffering of life … not a pain free life but a deep rich abundant life. Accepting the facts is more than a passive endurance of pain. It is also a decisive turning from a pre-occupation with personal comfort, convenience and pleasure. It is as we accept and even embrace the reality of suffering that we come to know and understand God's working in us.

It is in the real finite struggles of life that an infinite God reveals his love, grace, and power to us as well as to those around us. Skye Jethani, in *The Divine Commodity*, quotes Dallas Willard, "We are not to try to get in a position to avoid trials. And we are not to 'catastrophize' and declare the 'end of the world' when things happen." Jethani goes on to say, "the trials of ordinary existence are the divine curricula for spiritual maturity. These are the laser beams God uses to put our old self, with its misappropriated desires, to death and then resurrect a new self with new desires focused on a more lasting joy." In other words, although I really prefer comfort and a painless existence … that is neither my deepest need nor the way of greatest happiness. My greatest joy is in facing the trials with the empowerment, grace, inner strength and joy of a practical relationship with a personal God.

The first aspect of a faith response is to Face the Facts. With God's help, grace, and strength we can indeed face the real world through Christ who strengthens us.

2

ACCEPT THE FEELINGS

"Do not be terrified, do not be discouraged ..."

Praise the Lord!

Old brother Demoranville was one of the saints of the church. I'm sure he had a first name, but I never remember hearing it out loud. Whenever the church doors were open he would be there. Wednesday was prayer meeting night, and as usual he was there. Prayer meeting was a time of singing, corporate prayer, as well as shared personal testimonies.

Brother Demoranville was a builder and apparently was building a shed in his back yard when he smashed his thumb with a hammer. He went into some detail describing his bruised, busted, bloody thumb and credited God's grace for his saintly response. Jumping up and down in pain, holding his injured thumb, crying out Praise the Lord – Praise the Lord – Praise the Lord! I remember being duly impressed with such godliness and enjoyed the story greatly as well.

I, however, have not nearly approached that level of sainthood. If I smash my thumb, I will be full of spiritual pride if I *don't* say some of the words I shouldn't out loud. When life shakes you up, when bad news comes into your life, you will not feel good about the situation. And we *shouldn't* feel good about bad news because, and the response applies again … duh … bad news is BAD.

Battle Plan from the General

Look again at Joshua the warrior, now politician/priest/babysitter.   God spoke to Joshua saying, "Have I not commanded you? Be strong and courageous. Do not be terrified; do not be discouraged, for the Lord your God will be with you wherever you go." *(Joshua 1:9)*

Why did God have to tell Joshua, this tough battle hardened veteran, don't be terrified or discouraged? It had something to do with the fact that he felt terrified and discouraged ... he had to admit and accept the feelings. Joshua would have a deep sense of sorrow and loss. He was the *general* but Moses was the *"commander in chief,"* in an Israeli nomadic kind of way. At times we view biblical characters as though they were so spiritual that they had no feelings. Joshua would have known all of the feelings expected of one who was facing overwhelming challenges. His good friend and leader was dead. He was entering a land of warriors who were so massive that the scouts returned feeling as though "we were grasshoppers in their sight." As a military leader, Joshua understood that a soldier would have needed to keep his emotions under control in order to be effective. It was not routine for Joshua to face new and difficult emotional challenges.

In the unexpected, painful, traumatic times of life the feelings of anger, fear, doubt, and despair can be overwhelming. The temptation is real to believe that because we are Christian ... living by faith ... trusting God ... we should not have these kinds of feelings. The reality is that the emotions we would rather avoid are God's gifts which draw us into a deeper understanding of his grace-full working in our lives. In other words, we are able to experience more of God's love and strength as we accept the help of his grace.

Accept the Feelings

The way of Christ is a way of great joy. There is within Christian circles, however, a combination of misconception and misrepresentation that produces a false appearance of joy, or at least linguistic and facial pleasantness. The misconception is that Christians never stop smiling. This distortion of reality is reinforced ... by the smiling Christians on television, the pastor who is always "up" every Sunday (you should see the same pastor on Monday morning), and by the false application of scripture. So often Christians bear the burden of an unrealistic expectation that living their faith includes being strong and happy, whatever life brings their way.

The result is a façade that ensures that no one is allowed to see their broken heart. When there is death, don't deny the sorrow. When there's injustice, don't pretend there is no anger. When you are weak don't pretend you are not discouraged. Be a real person. For many Christians a new act debuts each week. The marquee proclaims in lights: "I'm okay ... You're okay ... Don't ask me any different."

Broken hearts are so often camouflaged by "Sunday go to meeting clothes" and a hearty handshake. Christians are too busy to be real. Do we allow Christians in our fellowship to be sad? Do we allow them to go through times of fear without judging their spirituality? Perhaps a more personal question is; do you allow *yourself* to be sad? Do you allow *yourself* to be fearful?

Accept the feelings. Feel the feelings. God gave you feelings to help identify areas of need in your life. If you *feel* tired, you need rest. If you *feel* sorrow, you need to mourn. If you *feel* lonely, you need a friend. Feelings are used by God as tools to bring healing and compassion. Henry Nouwen speaks of God's working of grace in times of crisis:

> Every time you experience the pain of rejection, absence, or death, you are faced with a choice. You can become bitter and decide not to love again, or you can stand straight in your pain and let the soil on which you stand become richer and more able to give life to new seeds.

(The Voice of Inner Love)

Nouwen speaks of a faith-choice ... we can become bitter in our pain, or we can stand straight in our pain. Bitterness is a *decision* not to love again. Faith is a *decision* to stand strong, trusting God and allowing the soil of our pain, sorrow, and loss to nurture the growth of new seeds of grace and serenity. The admonition of scripture calls us to a decision of faith to stand strong drawing on the resources of God.

> Finally, be strong in the Lord and in his mighty power. Put on the full armor of God so that you can take your stand against the devil's schemes. For our struggle is not against flesh and blood, but against the rulers, against the authorities, against the powers of this dark world and against the spiritual forces of evil in the heavenly realms. Therefore put on the full armor of God, so that when the day of evil comes, you may be able to stand your ground, and after you have done everything, to stand. (*Ephesians 6:10-13*)

Feelings denied, repressed, or ignored become psycho-spiritual toxins that saturate every aspect of life. Unrecognized feelings of pain and trauma have a devastating effect on our relationship with God, relationships with others, as well as our personal integrity and serenity. Don't pretend. Pretending isolates the real you from those who can help and care for you. Maintaining a façade takes great resources that are needed for facing life head on.

In the days, months and years following my diagnosis of Parkinson's disease, I experienced feelings and emotions with an intensity I had never known before. It just wasn't like me to be so overwhelmed on the emotional level. I was and am the strong silent type, which if truth be told is closer to denial than strength. As I look back on my journal I am reminded of the impact of hurt, pain and sorrow on the feeling level.

The following is a journal entry, as I faced the reality, that soon I would no longer be the pastor of a local congregation. From time to time, I would be teased about my notebooks, lists and charts, which I used as tools in church planning and leadership training. I found these strategies and tools helpful even if my leaders were rather bemused with my methodology.

September 8, 2004

I'm looking through a notebook of my lists, charts, and my bright ideas. I am slowly letting them all go. It begins to feel like mourning, losing so much of what I love so deeply. I don't love the lists. I do love the lives and the people and the "calling" all those lists and flailing efforts in ministry represent.

Everything I am draws me to immerse myself in the work of God and in his people. But the thing I love the most brings such confusion and weariness. I'm so sad to think about losing my people. They're not really my people, they are God's people, but they are so entwined with my heart, and I have grown to lean upon them in my time of need. Tears would help. It's like the sorrow is too deep for tears. Tears are not my gift.

It was crucial to accept the reality of the emotional impact of devastating news. At times Christians act as though they are above the feelings of fear, loneliness and despair. We are made in the image of God and even Jesus himself knew fear, anger, frustration, loneliness ...

***

Elisabeth Kubler-Ross in her book "On Death and Dying" contributed a helpful, now familiar to most, model as a template in understanding the emotions of those facing death or loss.

The Five Stages of Grief Model:

Denial - A conscious or unconscious refusal to accept facts which insulates a person from the impact of a traumatic experience.

Anger - Feelings of wanting to strike out at anything responsible for personal pain. This can include people, circumstances, fate, God etc.

Bargaining - Attempts to make a deal with God or compromise to resolve a negative, hurtful, or unfair situation.

Depression - Feelings of sadness, regret, fear, uncertainty etc.

Acceptance - Finding a peace about the pain of life along with some understanding of how to face personal pain and difficulties.

It is not my purpose to delve too deeply into the sociology/psychology of Elisabeth Kubler Ross, but her model is helpful to us. The Kubler-Ross model was never presented as a linear step by step method of coping but rather a framework for helping those facing the difficult realities of life and death. Her point was that there is no five step program for getting the mourning out of the way and check it off your list. When life hits you hard, it is likely that you would experience some, or all of these aspects of adjustments and feelings and understanding them is helpful.

When the unexpected strikes, there will be feelings that are so intense they threaten to cripple any attempts at responding with faith.

Sorrow and Loss

As I mentioned, I am not prone to over-emotionalism. Partly I was reacting to growing up in a church that at times was more than a little emotional and manipulative. Mostly, however, I was raised in New England and tend to be somewhat introverted by nature. I rarely cried and do not remember ever having a good old fashioned sobbing "cry."

I was preaching to the chairs in the sanctuary of the church where I was the pastor. This was part of my weekly sermon preparation, and they were great chairs ... attentive chairs ... they never criticized. Basically I would try to listen to the sermon, and if I was too bored myself, maybe make some changes.

All of a sudden it struck me that "it was all over." I began to weep, as I never had before. I had been trying so hard to continue in ministry. Each week the typical schedule of preaching, teaching and interacting with people was a struggle. During the week, I was doing half as much as before diagnosis ... in twice the time. I was exhausted, feeling inadequate and totally drained. The conclusion was brutally evident: pastoral ministry was no longer an option.

We had been in our church for fourteen years, our kids had grown up there, the church was healthy, I was healthy ... it was home. The call to pastoral ministry had never faded. Never once did I wake up on the infamous clergy "Monday morning" and think "I'm ready to quit." But all that was over. I would never be a pastor again. I would never preach again. I would have to leave my church family. So much of what I loved was gone. It was all over. For three hours I wept and wept ... mourning the loss ... crying out to God.

Don't be afraid of tears; they are a gift from God. I needed to feel those feelings. The inner pain, stress, and struggle needed to come out. The tears were healing tears. There was a peace and acceptance that came with the tears. When life and circumstances seem to conspire against us, we need to deal with the emotions that will inevitably be part of a response of faith.

Anger

Anger is an emotion that many Christians struggle with. "Gimme that old time religion," the old song says … "makes me love everybody." When blind-sided by tragedy, when a trust is betrayed, when people strike out in cruelty … it doesn't make me feel like loving everybody. Christians at times feel like they are something less than spiritual when they experience anger and frustration.

I felt somewhat less than spiritual as I faced my nemesis of PD. I was puzzled and upset. I was angry. Why would God allow a faithful pastor, wannabe athlete, humorous, very bright, and extremely humble person, to get Parkinson's disease? It doesn't make sense. It certainly wasn't my idea. What possible good can come from an early retirement in the prime of my life, just when I was finally able run circles around those old guys at the alumni basketball game?

I didn't really understand what God was doing, but I didn't really go too far down the "angry with God" road. Perhaps I believed in the benevolent nature of a personal God after all. Past observation made it clear to me that God didn't rely on me to spell check his omnipotent, omniscient, infinite plans and workings. We will later deal with doubting and questioning of God. The target for my anger was more the disease than God … fate … luck or whatever. I projected a persona on my disease; the bad breathed salesman. Following are a few journal entries:

April 24, 2003

> *The challenge comes when I go to sleep and wake up with the stiffness and discomfort of a disease that pushes its way into my life. The disease rudely butts into my schedule, like an annoying salesman with bad breath … like that dysfunctional person you avoid but they show up in your bedroom at 4:30 AM. What do you do with a bothersome guest trespassing in your life? No matter how rude I am with this intruder … Always there. See what happens? The challenges and hurt of life will break in and pollute your thoughts and take your soul.*

April 26, 2003

> *It's five o'clock in the morning, and I can smell the bad breath. It's that salesman again. He's handing out free samples of achy stiffness. It seems to shake me up more each day.*

May 12, 2003

>*I have hung up on the salesman, told him I'm not interested . . . that his mother wears army boots ... he just doesn't quit. I took the phone off the hook last night, but he pushed his way in again. Nothing real extreme, just enough to torment. Pins and needles, nagging pains, stiffness, just enough to take away my sleep.*

>*He is selling mind altering drugs tonight. I'm not buying, but somehow I can't say no to his offer of loneliness and fear. Loneliness seems to be a recurring theme. Getting rid of the salesman will take more than rudeness. I need to go to battle with the help of God, and all the resources he has provided.*

May 28, 2003

>*Here he comes again. You know its halitosis Harry the salesman... his teeth are crooked... he dresses funny... his mother wears army boots... but he is persistent and he always seems to sell some of his merchandise. It's almost like I can't resist and the list seems to get longer each time he visits.*

I was sick and tired of that salesman and all that he was selling. Things in life that we are unable to change … things that are unfair … painful … frustrating … can destroy our faith and pollute our lives with a self-absorbed discontent that expresses itself in anger.

Again, my purpose is not to provide an in-depth study of the nature, source, and response to anger, but rather, to emphasize the importance of accepting the feelings that are a natural human reality in times of crisis. Feelings are real. We need to deal with them.

The serenity prayer is about the best initial response in times of anger and frustration:

God, grant me the serenity to accept the things

I cannot change; the courage to change the things

I can; and the wisdom to know the difference.

Confusion

I have always tried and perhaps even prided myself in thinking well and planning ahead. The commitment to serving, leading and ministry was strengthened by a sense of knowing *what* I was doing and *why* I was doing it. Time spent seeking a personal vision from God, followed by thinking and planning as to how this vision could be implemented was perhaps my most important focus as a pastor. This vision was then modified and clarified in tandem with the local leadership with the goal of sharing a vision to implement together. A shared vision was foundational to any pastoral authority I might exercise.

As my disease progressed it became more and more difficult to think well enough or clearly enough to offer effective leadership to my church. The focus more and more was upon survival rather than mission. Disability and resignation/retirement reared their ugly heads. As if the inability to think clearly wasn't bad enough, I was required to provide documentation certifying my 'dim witted-ness' for Social Security.

As I look back over some of the documents, I read my wife's observations of my growing disability. She wrote of "an increased insecurity in Ken's ministry and confidence in interfacing with people ... he has cut down his work schedule, trying to work productively for one- two hours a day ... in his productive time he is not able to field three questions asked in a row ... the physical symptoms are a factor in Ken's inability to work, but the most distressing are those that affect his mind, and his ability to do simple tasks that were once so easily accomplished."

It is still very difficult to accept the cognitive limitations.

Another journal entry:

October 23, 2004

> *I've seen God use lots of nut cases in amazing ways. I am praying that if my brains are scrambled, that Jesus would shine through anyway. People have loved us so much. I don't want to disappoint them. But it is tearing me apart to try to lead and be unable to do so. Perhaps it*

is time for all of us to release what is to God's care. I am not ready to be different than I am.

***

A great quote from devotional writer Bertha Munro; in Christ we can face life *"not somehow but triumphantly."* I do believe that but along with the *yin* of spiritual triumph, I have known the *yang* of getting through … not triumphantly, but somehow.

Loneliness

I really am a nice guy. I like people. I enjoy fellowship. But I enjoy the alone times as well and have experienced the occasional attack of home sickness. While in seminary in Kansas City, I had more than once wanted to turn onto I-70 homeward bound to the east instead of west. I have followed a car with a Massachusetts license plate in Prince Albert, Saskatchewan Canada to a bar where a traveling rock band was playing. Once or twice I even called the directory assistance to hear the Boston accent I had grown up with. (I had stopped speaking as a Bostonian, mostly because my Canadian friends teased me mercilessly when I spoke my "native tongue.") For the most part, however, I have been okay with alone time.

Loneliness was a new experience for me. Loneliness will necessarily be a part of any crisis situation. In a certain sense there are aspects of sorrow, abuse, fear, anguish that will be faced alone with God.

November 3, 2004

> *I have been more loved and cared for than ever before ... And lonelier than ever before. God is so good; because of his love and grace he is there in the lonely times. I look into the eyes of those I love, and I can see how much they want to enter into the lonely room with me but there's only room for one. We sent our kids off to kindergarten with tears, and they got on the bus alone. I'm not sure I want to stay on this bus.*

> *I am alone.*

> *What is it about being alone? There is some kind of insecurity thing happening here. To remember at Camp Idlewild, a beautiful island on a New Hampshire lake. It might have been my first year at camp. I cried myself to sleep. My dad was chaplain, he was close by. My big brother, the protector no one messed with, was there to teach me the ropes. I knew I was okay. But everything around was unfamiliar, and I was lonely for the security of familiar surroundings.*

> *Many things around me now are unfamiliar. I don't move the same, feel the same, or speak the same. My mind strays away from the familiar pattern of logical*

analysis and intentional response. Brenda and I have a marriage with which we are unfamiliar. We are not used to the dependency that is now part of my life on the feeling level. It boggles my mind to face an unfamiliar role in my church. I am alone, surrounded by the unfamiliar.

***

It's important to understand that in our time of crisis people will not really "get" what we are going through, whatever the situation:

> … When a parent is overwhelmed, sleepless, fearful, and exhausted with a new born infant … *the laughing response is "this is the easy part… wait until they are teenagers!"*

> … When I am ripped apart having to accept my disability … *the inconsiderate response is "what in the world do you do with all your time?"*

> … When one is betrayed by a spouse ….*the automatic response is "don't worry time heals."*

> … When my mind is so confused sometimes … *the easy response is "I am exactly the same way, I forget too."*

These responses to your crisis are loving, caring, and thoughtless. People really do care, but they don't know what to say. Often people will say nothing when faced with the crisis of another. Much of our personal pain and trauma is faced alone.

Decide ahead of time to be kind with people who don't "get" it. For the most part they mean no harm. Henri Nouwen speaks of this loneliness:

> Much of our isolation is self-chosen. We do not like to be dependent on others and, whenever possible, we try to show ourselves that we are in control of the situation and can make our own decisions. This self-reliance has many attractions. It gives us a sense of power, it allows us to move quickly, it offers us the satisfaction of being our own boss, and it promises many rewards and prizes. However, the underside of self-reliance is loneliness, isolation, and the constant fear of not making it in life. *(Here and Now)*

Depression

The lonely times are often accompanied by feelings of depression. My regular neurologist appointment was scheduled every three months in Manhattan. My neurologist kept telling me he thought I was depressed. To be totally honest, he didn't *think* I was depressed, he said that I *was* depressed. For several months my response was, "No I'm not."

He didn't understand that my understated and boring demeanor was all part of the mix of characteristics of my unique and special persona. It was one of the endearing qualities that made me ... *me*. I tend toward deadpan humor ... boring has served me well. If I did feel down, I could always read the Psalms, pray, go catch a fish, or eat a hot fudge sundae. I knew how to handle the low times.

For several appointments, we did the "are to" … "am not" … "are to" … "am not" routine after which he prescribed a pill. I did not like taking another pill, especially for depression. There just seems to be something self-focused, self-serving, and weak about feeling mopey, (which is a clinical term even if my spell check doesn't recognize it.) I didn't know which was worse, being depressed or having to take a pill for depression. The whole thing was depressing! Looking back at my journal entries it is clear that dealing with depression was an ongoing process:

May 25, 2002

> *It's three o'clock in the morning again. The depression pills are working well because I'm pretty depressed. It looks like the second evil purple pill complicates my sleeping patterns with its contribution of insomnia. However, my body got used to the first pill so I suppose it will get used to the toxicity of the second pill as well. Hopefully the others 18 pills will cooperate in helping me toward one of the more basic goals... survival.*

The fact remains that 33 to 35 million people struggle with depression in the United States. The World Health Organization estimates that over 121 million people suffer from depressive symptoms worldwide. In certain ways, feelings of depression are a natural response to injury, hurt and pain …remember the "bad news feels bad" principle? Depression.com (why do I find

Depression.com amusing?) lists causes of depression such as genetics, trauma, negativity, physical disease and mental illness. Repressed anger as well is often an underlying origin of clinical depression. More than we'd like to admit, anger and depression are often related. Dr. Paul Meier of Meier Clinics once reported that approximately 15,000 Americans come in one week to the Minirth Meier Clinics for insight-oriented therapy. Of all the depression cases, he finds that 95% are depressed due to repressed anger toward an abuser or toward oneself. (We will look at the struggle between anger and forgiveness in the *Live the Faith* chapter.)

There are practical life style responses to depression including:

Exercise. Regular exercise provides natural, mood lifting chemical changes in your body. You don't have to train for a marathon; even a short walk every day will help.

Nutrition. Eating a regular, balanced diet is important for both your physical and mental health.

Sleep. Poor sleep has a strong effect on mood. Make getting the right amount of sleep for you a priority. I also swallowed my pride and took a sleeping pill.

Social Support. Strong social networks reduce isolation, a key risk factor for depression. Keep in regular contact with friends and family, or consider joining a class or group. Volunteering is a wonderful way to get social support and help others while also helping yourself.

Stress Reduction. Make changes in your life to help manage and reduce stress. Too much stress exacerbates depression and puts you at risk for future depression.

Medication. Don't feel guilty about medication. Half of all Parkinson's patients deal with depression. Regardless of the root causes of depression there are actual brain changes including the reduction of serotonin and dopamine. If medication is a help, thank God and take your meds.

Again, my purpose is not a clinical study of stress, trauma, depression etc. But rather to emphasize that when life shakes us up, feelings happen. These feelings need to be recognized, addressed, and accepted as an unavoidable and maybe even indispensable part of struggling with troubling and turbulent real life experiences.

Doubt

Doubt is the feeling … faith is the choice.

"If you have faith as small as a mustard seed," Jesus says, "you can say to this mountain, 'Move from here to there' and it will move. Nothing will be impossible for you." (*Matthew 17:20*)

Why is that less than encouraging to most of us? How many have tossed mountains around? What's more, mountain tossing doesn't even take very much faith … only as much as an itty bitty seed. Does that make you feel like a spiritual pygmy?

And to top it all off, we aren't even allowed to doubt.

"I tell you the truth, if anyone says to this mountain, 'Go, throw yourself into the sea,' and does not doubt in his heart but believes that what he says will happen, it will be done for him." (*Mark 11:23*)

"And he did not do many miracles there because of their lack of faith." (*Matthew 13:58*)

"'Go,' said Jesus, 'your faith has healed you.' Immediately he received his sight and followed Jesus along the road." (*Mark 10:52*)

We want to have faith … we want to believe … but the doubt just won't go away. How can a God of love allow such pain, struggle, and tragedy?

Take a look at God's response to doubters.

Job was the perfect man, yet he was stricken with unspeakable pain and tragedy. He had more than a few doubts as he challenged God saying basically, what in the world are you doing? God's first response was patience. He listened to

Job's complaint. The almighty infinite God, sat down with a rancher (if you will excuse the anthropomorphism) to listen to what he had to say.

There were some things that Job just didn't get ... so God responded with a litany questions for Job, the first of which is *Job 38:4-6* "Where were you when I laid the earth's foundation? Tell me, if you understand." Job's response? "...Surely I spoke of things I did not understand, things too wonderful for me to know." Job was reminded that God is God and there are some things too awesome and wonderful for him to fully understand. The fact remains that doubt will happen. There will be aspects of our suffering that we will not fully understand.

***

The first things we did upon receiving the diagnosis of Parkinson's was to pray for divine healing. The instruction in the book of James is for those who are sick to "... call the elders of the church to pray over him and anoint him with oil in the name of the Lord. And the prayer offered in faith will make the sick person well; the Lord will raise him up. If he has sinned, he will be forgiven." *(James 5:14-15)*. I have been blessed beyond measure by those who have prayed for my healing. It is one of the many blessings I would not have known if the "bad breathed salesman" had not knocked on my door.

It was perhaps the most humbling, praiseful, thankful day of my Christian life. Shortly after my diagnosis, several of my fellow pastors in the Metro New York City had come together; gathering their leaders to pray for my healing. They traveled to my suburban church north of New York City in the beautiful Hudson Valley. I was overwhelmed as nearly one hundred people made their way on a Sunday afternoon to join the congregation in my local church family to pray for healing. I was blown away by all the love and care and attention.

We assembled in the sanctuary and began to pray ... and there was faith in that room! For an hour and a half the prayers of faith were offered to a loving personal God. The diversity was a joy to behold as Asian, Hispanic, Caribbean, and Caucasian brothers and sisters prayed and praised God together. There was a fair amount of bad "name it ... claim it" type theology bandied about that day, but there was no lack of faith. There were 150 in one room agreeing together.

The end of the service came. I was not healed. What's with that? We had met the "requirements." There certainly must have been at least a **mustard** seed's worth of faith among such an earnest group. There had to be at least a few men or women righteous enough to qualify as that righteous one whose prayer ... "availeth much." *KJV*

In my struggles with the "whys" of my particular condition; there are three spiritual realities that have helped me.

God is Real

It takes little faith to believe that God is real. Even those who claim no particular faith recognize there is an "otherness." There is some kind of order that is somehow at the core of existence. Through our senses, we observe a few miraculous stunning mind boggling events in our lives and in our universe. Even the observations of the infinitesimal speck of creation/eternity within our awareness lead us to *know* that God is real. There is something out there ... meaning above us ... over us ... all transcendent.

Intuitively our souls reach out for that something more. September 11, 2001 was an unforgettable day of mayhem and tragedy. Living close to New York City brought the reality literally just next door. All around the world, the images flashed with the immediate instinctive response ... "Oh God!!!" We are created in the image of God with a natural inclination toward Him.

God is God ... which means we don't have to do the job. The position is filled. There are no layoffs in sight. As Christians our faith is built upon Jesus as the perfect revelation of the creator God. Jesus said, "If you have seen me you have seen the Father," *(John 14:9)* I'm not quite sure how heretical it is ... but somehow I think that Jesus might have left out a few things. He skipped the quantum physics classes to fully explain creation. Just exactly how did God sit down at His work bench and come up with my granddaughter's amazing blue eyes? Did God really keep count when he scattered the stars that bear testimony to my place in the universe?

God is God. He is in charge.

God is Love

Here is where faith comes in. Jesus understood the incapacity of humanity to comprehend the totality of the infinity of God. Jesus came not to reveal all the mysteries of God but rather to reveal his character. In this He held nothing back. Jesus came, giving his life away. He came to love his creation, literally, to death. God, in Christ, comes all the way down to share the joy, fear, and frustration of humanity. He understands the 'lostness' of alienation from the Father. God reaches out to us.

Faith is not the ability to know everything but rather it is establishing those things which are solid, upon which a life is built. In times of doubt, the response of faith is to re-confirm the reality that God loved the world so much that he sent Jesus, his one and only son. He reminds us and brings an inner confirmation of the loving nature of God.

God is love. God is for us.

God is at Work

How often do we hear the platitude, "God is in control?" The fact remains that God is not always in control of every occasion and situation in our world. Each individual can decide to rebel over God's control. The foundational principle is not as much God is in control, as that "God is at Work."

Romans 8:28 says that in all things God is at work for good. This verse can be glibly quoted in a "don't worry, God is in charge" kind of way. I don't want to hear that God is the Willy Wonka man upstairs, doling out personal miseries upon His creation. I kind of want the man upstairs to be a jolly, Santa-like, let me tell you a story, kind of God.

Again, I don't understand all about the meaning and purpose of pain and suffering, but I do know that we all face it. At this point, my faith in God through Christ is that his character is love and that he is at work for our benefit. When I am weak, God is at work bringing inner strength. When I am fearful, God is at work bringing comfort.

These three principles ... God is Real, God is Love, and God is at Work. These are the three interlocking foundation stones of faith.

God is Real ... is a foundation stone established by reason, observation, and revelation. God is Love ... is a leap of faith that Jesus Christ is the son of God and that he does indeed reveal to us the character of God. God is at Work ... is a foundation stone established by the revelation of scripture, history, and personal experience. Jesus Christ, the son of God is the center and cap stone supported by the other two tenets of faith.

In order to live out faith, we must have a foundation that is not easily shaken. Although feelings of doubt are part of our humanity they are not the basis upon which we make decisions for life.

We will never know all things:

But we must establish those things upon which

we base our decisions and actions of life.

Not one of us is exempt from the storm clouds of life. The good news is that we can live out a practical, and yes, even victorious life, as we make faith decisions. By faith, with the help of God, in relationship with him we can Face the Facts then Accept the Feelings of fear, doubt, anger and frustration, knowing that a loving creator God is at work in our behalf. It is vital that we grow up and face reality and accept that things are not always good, fair, or pleasant. But there is more than just a negative resolve to tough it out. Along the way we need to Count our Blessings.

3

COUNT THE BLESSINGS

"I will give you everyplace where you set your foot. . ."

The Last Christmas

Digger Phelps is a well known, often controversial sports analyst. For many years, he was highly successful as the coach of Notre Dame Basketball. Following coaching he was very active politically serving as part time ambassador and as director of President George H. W. Bush's anti-drug program. His autobiography, *The Son of an Undertaker*, is set in a neighboring small town of Beacon, New York.

He tells the story of his mother, well known as Maggie all around town. She was apparently quite a lively personality and involved in every aspect of the community. Digger's brother Francis was handsome, popular and a star basketball player on the high school team. It was assumed he would continue his success at the college level.

As a senior in high school, however, he contracted a freak infection from, of all things, a blood blister and died suddenly, a few days before Christmas. It was a tragedy for the family and for the community. From that year on, in response to this crushing loss, there would be no Christmas celebration in the Phelps household.

Every year in a community filled with hope, joy and Christmas cheer … the Phelps household was an island of mourning and despair. The darkness of sorrow and loss were window shades, shutting out the light of hope and peace. The blessings of *"for God so loved the world he sent his one and only son" (John 3:16)* were all around them, but they were unable to see them.

When life shakes us up, it is easy to be overwhelmed with the intensity and stress that permeates every moment, thought, and plan. The path of least resistance is always there. We become so focused on the trial that we lose sight of the blessings. A quarter, when held close to one eye with the other eye closed, will totally block off sight. As we move the quarter to arms length, however, away from ourselves, we are then able to see the entire environment around us. The quarter (trial) is still very much in focus, but along with the trial are the blessings of life … the light of day … the beauty of creation … the presence of those who love and support us.

When life shakes us up, the pain and discomfort so strongly wrench our attention away from the blessings that we lose sight of them all together. The truth is there is much more to reality than the present problem. The blessings are just as real ... perhaps even more real.

When the struggle and strain of life becomes overwhelming, that is the time to make a decision to not only Face the Facts ... and Accept the Feelings, but to Count our Blessings as well. Let's look at our Israeli general again.

Battle Plan from the General

Joshua needed to Face the Facts; Moses was dead. He needed to Accept the Feelings; he was terrified and discouraged. The general needed as well to Count his Blessings. The voice of God comes to Joshua with great promise and blessing:

> I will give you every place where you set your foot, as I promised Moses. Your territory will extend from the desert to Lebanon, and from the great river, the Euphrates--all the Hittite country--to the Great Sea on the west. No one will be able to stand up against you all the days of your life. As I was with Moses, so I will be with you; I will never leave you nor forsake you. (*Joshua 1:3-5*)

Joshua faced an insurmountable challenge but at the same time... the blessings of God were still both visible and available. There would be bloodshed, sorrow and loss. The battles would be brutal. The victories would come at great cost. There would be rebellion among the people. But all of this did not change the reality of God's blessings. In the midst of all the turmoil ... there was more than trial and trauma. God was still the God of Abraham, Isaac, and Jacob. The promise for victory and the divine pledge that Joshua would never be alone had not changed. It is important and indispensible to count the blessings of life.

Personal

The words used to describe PD are rather ominous. Among them are devastating, debilitating, progressive, and incurable. More and more, I have been able to do less and less. I spent 10 to 12 hours with a clinical psychologist trying to figure out what in the world was happening with my brain. There were tests for reading comprehension, vocabulary, numerical sequence, name the presidents backwards (getting stuck at Bush Sr.). There were the arithmetic word problems that literally confirmed I was not smarter than a 5th grader. The good news is that I still scored in the 95th percentile in some of the academic areas. The not as good news is that I scored from 37th down to 10th percentile in short term memory, multitasking, facial recognition and problem solving type tests. It was not exactly a pretty picture.

The official diagnosis was progressive Parkinsonian Dementia. (Please Note: Any significant repetition in this book is because I can't quite remember what I wrote). That D word stood out on the psychological report like a neon light. And in case there was any illusion of returning to ministry the final note in the report was a recommendation that "Rev. Ardrey not work at all." It was enough to make me feel sorry for myself ... which occasionally was and is my response.

I was indeed devastated by the physical, emotional, and cognitive losses of PD. I had always done the family finances. As hard as I tried I couldn't avoid the costly over draft late bill type errors. Giving up the role of taking charge in that area came with a big gulp of swallowed pride.

I didn't like watching others do "my" work in "my" church.

Our church gained a new understanding of the "every member a minister" program. How blessed we had been with a secretary, administrator, youth pastor, finance committee, building committee and many others who did so much of the pastoral work during the time I struggled with an impending resignation and retirement. Important things were left un-done ... things I would have, could have, and should have done. The families moving into 800 new homes built so close to our church were not welcomed into the community. The Living Nativity, a long held tradition in the community didn't quite happen. People in the church were so faithful, but so much happened that was reactive, and the sense of moving forward in a pro-active manner was lacking. I was called to be a pastor ... specifically with this group of people in this setting. The need for effusive praise or validation was never high on my list of needs. But "I don't matter" kinds of feelings began to intrude upon my life. I wasn't "the" pastor any more. I wasn't consulted. It was pass in the keys to the church car then get on with life. It would have been easy to be overwhelmed by the bad news and miss the blessings of God which are new every morning.

"Facing the Facts" and "Accepting the Feelings" are important, indispensible decisions ... but they are dangerous. Dealing with disaster can easily become the groundwork of unhealthy cynicism, which is rich, fertile ground for a harvest of negativity and defeat. A recent letter to the editor in the Poughkeepsie, NY Journal is almost humorous if it wasn't so depressing.

> Human beings stink. (Why do I find *that* humorous?) We're caught up in our self-absorbed cocoons ... we pursue our mundane little lives. We hear about the Gulf Coast's oil saturated pelicans, the tortured burning turtles, the poisoned whales and dolphins. We eat our fast food, shake our heads and say "Isn't it a shame." Instead of angrily massing to save ourselves and our world, we stand around like fatted cattle waiting to be slaughtered . . . But our crimes, yours and mine, are by far the worst. We know what those in charge (politicians) are doing and why. And still we do nothing. Let's just drink another beer and watch our world die. Oh well.

Talk about Alexander and the Terrible, Horrible, No Good, Very Bad Day, Chicken Little, and Eeyore all coming together. Cynicism is a cancer that attacks our faith and blinds us to God's blessings and his available grace. In his book, *The Return of the Prodigal Son*, Henry Nouwen wrote:

Cynics seek darkness wherever they go. They point always to approaching dangers, impure motives, and hidden schemes. They call trust ... naïve; care ... romance; and forgiveness ... sentimental. They sneer at enthusiasm, ridicule spiritual favor, and despise charismatic behavior. They consider themselves realists who see reality for what it truly is and who are not deceived by "escapist emotions." But in belittling God's joy, their darkness only calls forth more darkness. *(The Return of the Prodigal Son)*

It is important to ask ourselves, "What are we looking for?" If we look for despair, we will find enough negativity to saturate our hearts and fill our lives with cynicism. If we look for the good around us, the blessings of God's grace, we will find our lives full of grace and hope.

Smile Through the Tears

Adeline Domingues was born in 1888 in the Cape Verde Islands to a devout Roman Catholic family. Adelina was also sincere and deeply committed to living a clean life and was very religious. As an eighteen year old young bride she was secretly reading the Bible on a hillside close to home, when all on her own she came to personal faith in Christ and was filled with joy and enthusiasm in her new found faith.

She had chosen the way of great struggle and opposition. She emigrated to the U.S. with her husband in 1907, and he worked as a fisherman in New Bedford, Massachusetts. Immediately she began looking for a church in the city asking, "Where is a good church, where people enjoy their religion?" She was directed to a small Church of the Nazarene, on the corner of Smith and Spruce Street, where she immediately became a vital part of their mission. The Portuguese Church of the Nazarene, later to become the International Church of the Nazarene, was established largely through her prayers, witnessing, preaching, and evangelism. She was on fire for God.

In all this time there was great criticism from the evangelical church for her fanaticism. There was vicious persecution from the old world Roman Catholic establishment in opposition to her proselytizing of the Catholic adherents. Her life was threatened, she was physically attacked, and she was ridiculed mercilessly. These were times of great pain and the temptation for discouragement was always there.

Adelina, known to me and my siblings as Mrs. Domingues, was one of the saints in the New Bedford church where my Dad was the pastor from 1960-1965. She was 75+ years old, even way back then. My Dad was an all out, working 80 hours a week, evangelistic pastor. Mrs. Domingues became his mentor. She understood the pain and joy of ministry, and as my Dad faced the pain and perhaps criticism of ministry, she would encourage him saying, "Brother Ardrey, with Jesus I have learned to smile through the tears." In pain and persecution, she never lost sight of the joy. When there were those in the church who just couldn't seem to keep strong in their faith she would smile and say, "Well, brother Ardrey, you know, some people you will just need to carry into heaven." She was able to see the blessing in the midst of even the most frustrating times. (*Living Stones in Africa: Pioneers of the Church of the Nazarene,* Paul S. Dayhoff)

The "on purpose" response of faith includes

a decision to Count the Blessings of life.

Look Around

Theologically the first decision needs to be "Look Up" to acknowledge the reality of the infinite presence of God. When we are all wrapped up in the survival mode of crisis, however, it is difficult to calm down and enjoy the serenity of metaphysical reflection. Sometimes all we can do is look around for something, anything that brings a glimmer of hope and optimism.

Begin small. Enjoy the obvious blessings closest to us. We can enjoy the sunshine, be thankful for the air we breathe, appreciate the beauty of nature around us. Express your observations of blessing in terms of gratitude to God. This is then a faith decision. In other words, the decision to be thankful reinforces our faith that God *is real*, strengthens our faith in his goodness, and confirms the reality that he is indeed at work and "delights to give good gifts to his children." (*Matthew 7:11*)

As we look around, the domain of blessing begins to expand. We begin to look beyond ourselves and the circumstances that threaten our very survival. Gratitude begins to grow into faith

habit; even perhaps a more daunting D-word, *discipline*. Henry
Nouwen speaks of the discipline of gratitude:

> In the past, I always thought of gratitude as a spontaneous
> response to the awareness of gifts received, but now I
> realize that gratitude can also be lived as a discipline. The
> discipline of gratitude is the explicit effort to acknowledge
> that all I am and have is given to me as a gift of love, a gift
> to be celebrated with joy. Gratitude as a discipline
> involves a conscious choice. I can choose to be grateful
> even when my emotions and feelings are still steeped in
> hurt and resentment. The choice for gratitude rarely comes
> without some real effort. But each time I make it, the next
> choice is a little easier, a little freer, a little less self-
> conscious. There is an Estonian proverb that says: "Who
> does not thank for a little will not thank for much." Acts
> of gratitude make one grateful because, step by step, they
> reveal that all is grace. (*The Return of the Prodigal Son*)

Make a decision to thank God for the small blessings. The
decision toward gratitude re-centers our prayers from a desperate
attitude of "Oh God help me" to a posture of "Oh God, thank you
for your blessings." The habit of gratitude transforms our time
spent with God. We are no longer coming to him, submitting a list
of complaints to the divine customer service department. We are
rather learning to commune with a loving God who blesses us in
our times of deepest need.

Look Upward

Those native to the northeast or northwest in the U.S. are
familiar with long stretches of dreary, sunless skies. My family and

I love the scenery of the northeast, dazzling in the fall ... green and lush in the summer. We love the ocean, spending weeks at a time on the Cape Cod National Sea Shore. However, we also endure some long stretches of sunless days.

In these periods of gloom there are times when the sky begins to brighten. Our heads instinctively turn upward in hope. When no one else can see a glimmer of light, my sunny optimistic wife will say, "It looks like the sun is coming out." Then when the sun breaks through we all look up and bask in the warmth and hopefulness of sunlight.

The habit of gratitude turns our attention upward. Gratitude expressed is both therapeutic and life changing. The decision to look around taking inventory of our many blessings is a first step. The next step is to look up to God as the source of the benefits we have received. As we turn our attention toward a transcendent but personal God, we are focused upon seeking after *him*, rather than seeking after his *answers*. Practicing gratitude as a discipline opens our minds and hearts to a God of goodness and grace.

Look Outward

National Geographic presented a documentary about the Hubbell telescope. The Hubbell telescope orbits around the earth probing far into the vast expanse of the universe. One striking image is that of a panorama of innumerable stars glittering on the screen in striking HD quality. Every one of those flickers of light was a galaxy. Every galaxy was composed of billions of stars. Every star had untold planets within its gravitational influence. It was totally mind boggling. The broadcast attempted to unravel the theoretical existence of black holes throughout the cosmos. As I understand it, a black hole is the central remaining core of an exploded star. A burning star, just as the molecular structure of earthly matter, is mostly space. Upon implosion all the mass is reduced to a miniscule sub atomic dot. All this concentrated mass, turned inward, exerts so much gravitational force that even light is unable to escape.

I don't get all that …but to me a star, totally turned inward and sucking the light out of the universe is an illustration. When cataclysmic unexpected events shake our lives with tragedy and trial, turning inward upon ourselves is the path of least resistance. Dr. Stan Toler, general superintendent of the Church of the Nazarene describes those people as those who curse, nurse, and rehearse their misfortunes. When we wallow in a pool of pity, the light of hope, faith and love is extinguished from our perception.

The need to look out … to look outside ourselves … is a decision to interface with the world around us and the people in it. Looking outward is a natural result of looking upward. Looking up in gratitude to God will tend to spill over into the world around us. When shaken by life, we can look outward *to* others for help and maybe more importantly *for* others who also need help and care. Even in pain and suffering it is possible to live a "grace-full" life and thus bring hope and faith into our world. The message of hope and grace can often be personally delivered more effectively in times of dis-ease than in times of ease. I never understood the paralysis of anxiety until my resources were stripped by disease, and I experienced for myself what it felt like to be overwhelmed and speechless when life gets too complicated.

Responding to these struggles, frustrations, and limitations is a dangerous affair. The potential for implosion into the black hole of self absorption is real. The potential is also there to look outward to those who really needed to see that faith in a loving, personal God is a practical, positive and possible decision.

Over the years, many have come to me with needs, fears, and concerns. My intention has always been to respond with care and compassion. I have tried to avoid a quick dismissive response and with God's help my responses have been mostly caring and transparent. A sympathetic response was fairly natural for me … at times; however, deep heart-felt empathy was perhaps less natural. Sometimes I just didn't "get it" how people were so crushed by seemingly minor concerns. I found myself empathizing with all my might but couldn't help thinking; "What's the big deal. Just deal with it!" Living with PD has brought new understanding and identification with those who have limited emotional and physical resources. I began to recognize blessings that I would not have known apart from my diagnosis. The following is a journal entry in the first year after the PD diagnosis:

February 2, 2001

Is it possible that I will be able to see God lead me into ministry and opportunities I never would have known without Parkinson's? I would have been too busy to write ... too pressured to enjoy family and friends ... Too hurried to be used by God to shed tears with those sent my way as a divine appointment. Maybe touching fewer people with greater impact because of that all surpassing power in a slowing, sometimes stumbling, often mixed up ... God seeker pastor ... That is from God ... As the resurrection turned the tables on Satan's worst. The power of God continues to turn the tables on the pain, tears, fear, and confusion of an evil disease ... That has opened the door to huge blessing. I have needed to rely on God's divine grace and security in a way that I never had before.

Gratitude

I am not often spiritual enough to thank God **for** my disease, but by faith even the suffering itself can be a blessing from God. In *The Hiding Place*, (a book every Christian should read) Corrie Ten Boom tells of her imprisonment in Ravensbrook concentration camp in Nazi Germany. Her arrival was a time of horrific fear and disgust:

> Our noses told us first that this place was filthy: somewhere plumbing had backed up, the bedding was soiled and rancid ...we saw that there were no individual beds at all but great square piers stacked three high

wedged side to side and end to end with only an occasional narrow aisle slicing through.

We followed our guide single file – the aisle was not wide enough for two – fighting back the claustrophobia of these platforms rising everywhere above us. At last she pointed to the second tier in the center of a large block. To reach it we had to stand on the bottom level, haul ourselves up, then crawl across three other straw covered platforms to reach the one that we would share with – how many ? The deck above us was too close to let us sit up. We lay back struggling against the nausea that swept over us from the reeking straw.

Suddenly I sat up, striking my head against the cross slats above. Something had pinched my leg.

"Fleas," I cried. "Betsie (her sister), this place is swarming with them … how can we live in such a place?"

Betsie began to pray … "Show us. Show us how."

They read a verse from the Bible smuggled in past the guards … "Give thanks in all circumstances." *(1 Thessalonians 5:18)* They began to thank God for every single thing about that place of total depravity. What a blessing that they were together with so many women closely packed in the barracks. They thanked God that the guards miraculously ignored the Bible that lifted their spirits. Betsie went on serenely, "Thank you for the fleas." – "The fleas!" Corrie said. "This was too much … there is no way even God can make me grateful for a flea."

In those unspeakable conditions, there was a nightly worship service where more and more women gathered for praise, prayer, and fellowship. The sisters would share the scripture in German and the message would be translated among the crowd into French, Russian, Polish, Czech and Dutch. The guards were a hostile presence every waking hour. But somehow, these precious worship times were never interrupted by the guards.

Sometime later there was a disagreement among the women, and the guards were called to settle it. Strangely, the guards refused to enter their barracks. Then it suddenly struck them that they were afraid of the fleas! It turned out that the fleas were keeping the guards away during the times of praise and worship. Without the fleas they would have been deprived of their greatest blessing and encouragement.

It is good advice and a wise strategy to look for the positive. When faced with the overwhelming and unexpected trauma it is important to face the facts and accept the feelings. But it is even more important to make an "on purpose" decision to:

Dwell on the positive and celebrate the blessings with gratitude.

Along the way we can count the blessings from God. The trials of life are real, but the promises of God are still sure. To really Face all the Facts we must Count the Blessings. Dealing with reality does not mean doom and gloom ... it includes recognizing the positive as well.

Michael J. Fox had it made. By the age of nineteen, he was the star of the popular family show *Family Ties*. The *Back to the Future* movies were blockbuster hits. He starred as well in the award winning sitcom *Spin City*. In 1980, he was diagnosed with PD at the age of twenty-nine.

Wealthy beyond that which most of us can imagine, he was beloved for his fun, likable characters in television and film. His life would certainly have been the envy of many. To the contrary, in his book *Lucky Man* he speaks of his way of life as the "Being-Famous-in-America-Fun House" lifestyle. He writes that, "It should come as no surprise that fame – show biz fame anyway – is so disorienting … after all the theater … is a conspiracy of mutual deception. The performer pretends to be someone he is not, and the audience willingly suspends its disbelief." (*Lucky Man*) In this world of 20 foot high screen characters, the actor is a matinee idol and a part of the viewer's family. "Everything is part of the show" – the performer's private life included. Within this topsy-turvy fun house of wavy mirrors, Michael J. Fox describes a world of alcohol and drug abuse, excess, family stress, entitlement and surprisingly, insecurity.

It was only as he received the worst news of his life … that he found his life. His diagnosis came at age twenty-nine! At forty-nine I was much too young, I thought, to have an old person's disease. If PD was bad news for me (at times crossing the line into devastating) then the life sentence for a twenty-nine year old would be more than devastating.

Fox found, however, that as he became part of the all out mission to cure Parkinson's disease, in giving to others, in working for a cause, he experienced joys he had never known. He found the peace that had previously been so elusive. He writes:

> If you were to rush into this room right now and announce that you had struck a deal with God, Allah, Buddha, Christ, Krishna, Bill Gates, whomever – in which the ten years since my diagnosis could be magically taken away, traded in for ten more years as the person I was before, I would, without a moment's hesitation, tell you to take a hike. The ten years since my diagnosis have been the best ten years of my life, and I consider myself a lucky man.

He wouldn't go back. Neither would I if I had to sell my soul to Bill Gates. Yet if there were a *legitimate* way to live the last ten years healthy ... count me in. Michael J. Fox has come to a faith that would not quite fit into the conservative evangelical Christian milieu, but his decision is a powerful example of a   life-changing, "on purpose" decision to seek and find the blessings that are always present in the darkest times.

But whatever the situation - we are people of hope. And as we count our blessings maybe we can lighten up a bit ... find some humor along the way. Often laughter is a positive alternative to despair. If we are to take life seriously we dare not take ourselves too seriously.

If we are to take life seriously we dare

not take ourselves too seriously.

I don't like the achy stiffness that is a grinding reality every day. I don't like the confusion when the medication wears off. There is an annoying woman who reminds me seven times a day to take my medicine; she resides in a micro chip in my pill box, and her voice persistently nags "time to take your pill – time to take your pill." But you know, I tell myself that it's not all bad.

One winter morning I was looking out my window at twenty-nine inches of snow in my driveway. I glanced at my son, just home from Kenya, with the unmistakable, wordless question in my eyes. "You expect me to shovel snow...in my condition?" Of course my son *graciously* shoveled the driveway without hesitation. Out of the kindness of their hearts (and to avoid a bit of manual labor) this past winter the kids bought my wife and I a snow blower.

It's not *all* bad.

I always thought that the Pastor Emeritus position was a pretty cool deal ... all the respect without the headaches. I didn't, however, plan to apply for the position at such a young age. Shortly after going on disability, sure enough, with the new pastor's arrival, I was installed as Pastor Emeritus. One evening, on a Wednesday family activity night, I was walking into the education building. As I made my way through the foyer, I heard a

81

familiar, (dare I say demanding voice) "Pastor! Pastor!" I turned my head immediately (because that's what pastors do ... having this messianic delusion of fixing anything and everything that may or may not need fixing). I heard the voice, turned my head and there was a presumptuously persistent (dare I say petulant) parishioner chasing the *new* pastor up the stairs. Again I said to myself, "I have some bad news in my life, but it's not *all* bad." Counting my Blessings was a bit easier that night.

We are people of hope. This life is not all there is. We have an eternal hope. At the risk of understating the gravity of the reality of death ... we can live with the ultimate hope.

A principle to live by:

Cheer up someday you are going to die!

My friend John was diagnosed with cancer of the eye a few years back. It was frightening news and as treatment was administered, we all thought that everything was OK. Within the year, however, the report was that the cancer was back, in his lymph nodes and even more ominously, in his liver. The doctors gave him 6-8 weeks to live.

John was with us for two more years. During those years he became a totally joy filled ambassador of the hope and joy of God's grace. Everywhere he went he spoke of the peace and joy he had come to know in relationship with a personal God. Traveling alone on the train to Philadelphia for the painful treatments of a clinical trial; he would share with fellow passengers how real God was in his life.

John would tell me, "these have been the best years of my life." And there is no way in the world I can really understand that. How does someone spend the best two years of his life dying? He had certainly recognized the blessings and was living out a life of gratitude.

***

Robert Schuler wrote a book entitled *Tough Times Don't Last but Tough People Do*. There is lots of good stuff in his book that strengthen resolve to toughen up, trust God, and deal with life. It is especially helpful when tough times don't last. But what about when tough times do last? I sent the *Tough Times* book to an acquaintance a number of years ago … and the tough times didn't last … they got worse. The financial pressure, taxes, family crises all brought increasing stress and strain.

When the going gets tough… the tough get going. There are those times when we feel anything but tough. In those times, part of an "on purpose" faith response is *Count the Blessings*. The premise of this book and the spiritual potential for all people of faith is that recognizing the blessings in the midst of the stress and strain and struggles of life *is* possible.

Years ago, a Canadian pastor's wife shared a memory from her childhood. She grew up in great poverty in the Peace

River country way up northwest of Edmonton, Alberta, Canada. She had been going to Sunday school and was so very sincere and enthusiastic in her growing faith. In her hunger, she would pray that God would supply the need for food each day. Her mother had died, and she was under the care of an aunt who was more skeptic than believer. There came a point in time when they had nothing left but one can of tomato soup. As the can was opened, they were horrified to see a big green worm in the soup.

The skeptical aunt sat right down and wrote an irate letter to the soup company, demanding a refund. Not many days after, a large box was delivered to their door step. In the box was a whole case of soups in various varieties from the company apologizing for their oversight.

The little girl was thrilled to see how God had provided for them. Excitedly she told her aunt how God had answered her prayers. Unconvinced, the well meaning but faithless aunt replied, "That was not God; that was me. I wrote the letter. The company was merely responding to a customer complaint." The "faith-full" child thought for a moment then responded, "That may be true ... but *who put the worm in the soup?*"

Looking for the good... practicing gratitude as a discipline is a decision of faith. When we get bad news - when life is unfair - when it seems hopeless ... don't stop living. Don't lose sight of the blessings. Nothing will ever shake the foundation stones of faith: God is Real ... God is Love ... God is at Work. God still loves the world so much he gave his one and only son that whoever believes in him shall not perish but have eternal life.

So stuff happens ... but when it does,

Face the Facts ... Accept the Feelings ... Count the Blessings ...

Live the Faith

4

LIVE THE FAITH

"Be careful to obey all the law my servant Moses gave you . . ."

Don't Just Sit There

My college years, the time span of 1968-1972, was the chronological epicenter of the Age of Aquarius. These were days of protest. We were protesting the Vietnam War; the hypocrisy of the previous generation; the legalism of our conservative denomination ... the list goes on and on. It was fun ... even mostly sincere.

During this time, our very popular Dean of Students was suddenly removed from his position without explanation. The bad news was that he was removed ... the good news was that it was a great legitimate (we thought) opportunity to protest. Something had to be done! The injustice which had been perpetrated on the masses by the monolithic, heartless establishment could not be tolerated! "Do not trust anyone over thirty!" was our mantra. And we knew for a fact that the Board of Trustees was infested with fossilized relics, some of whom had been tottering around this old earth for more than half a century.

The word was passed from conspirator to conspirator . . . the plan was to walk out of chapel in protest. The timing couldn't have been better because the chapel speaker was the representative embodiment of our overly conservative denomination ... the General Superintendant. His position topped the imperious, oppressive chain of command which had spawned the injustice which we were now enduring. The strategy was to walk out of chapel service as soon as the General Superintendant got up to speak.

The chapel that day was packed. Even those who had bribed their chapel checker, and didn't need to attend, were there. At the appointed time, the sound of squeaking pews and shuffling feet spread across the chapel as most of the students made their way to the exits. The General Superintendant rose to address the smattering of students left and announced his topic of the day. "The title of my message is" ... (pausing for effect) ... "Don't Just Sit There – Do Something!"

The temptation when the crises of life overwhelm us is to sit around and marinate in our misery. One of the indispensible elements of an "on purpose" faith response to the struggles that come our way is to make a decision to keep on living ... don't just sit there, do something, "Live the Faith."

Battle Plan from the General

Let's look again at Joshua the Israeli general. Joshua already had the expertise and experience to lead an army into battle, but God had called him to that which went above and beyond the nitty-gritty of planning and executing a military campaign. God's call to Joshua was a call to live out his faith in the God of Abraham, Isaac, and Jacob.

> Now then, (God says) you and all these people, get ready to cross the Jordan River into the land I am about to give to them--to the Israelites. I will give you every place where you set your foot, as I promised Moses ... be careful to obey all the law my servant Moses gave you; do not turn from it to the right or to the left, that you may be successful wherever you go. Do not let this Book of the Law depart from your mouth; meditate on it day and night, so that you may be careful to do everything written in it. Then you will be prosperous and successful. *(Portions of Joshua 1:1-8)*

Joshua needed to get up and get going in obedience to God's clear direction for him and his people. All of his success, strength, wisdom, and his very survival depended entirely upon his trust and faith in God. He not only needed to wage war ... he needed to live his faith.

Personal

When life shakes you up, it is not necessarily easier to live out your faith in everyday life. The pressures of the crisis, the emptiness of bereavement, the shock of unfaithfulness can so preoccupy our consciousness that we begin to lose sight of what we believe and how we are to live.

I had always taught and preached that my identity was not that of being a pastor, but rather my identity was and is found as a child of God. That was good preaching, and I believed it then as well as now. But I soon found out that although I was just as much a child of God after the diagnosis, I was and am no longer the same person. With change happening all around me, I needed to reconfirm my faith in a God who *is* Real ... a God who is Love ... and a God who is at Work.

The premise of this book is that we as people of faith need not lose hope when we are shaken by life. We need not follow the path of least resistance. Every Christian can make an "on purpose" faith decision to live out their faith. When shaken by life, we then choose the road to be followed. Below is a journal entry as I slowly walked the hundred yards from our church to the parsonage. Maybe it was the drugs I was taking, but it seemed that there were roads branching off one way and another. It seemed that there were choices set before me.

September 12, 2004

> *Walking across the field to home - I never noticed it before but it seemed at least two miles past right center*

field to "my" house ... which is also my home. I played the part well ... slowly, pensively, not quite tearfully... knowing where I was going ... wondering where I was going. Never noticed so many roads... must have been too busy to notice.

There were street signs. I read the signs seeking which direction to go. There was the road of fear. I took a look down the road... not that I'm afraid... scared spitless maybe but not afraid. There's another road - the road of faith ... I'm too afraid to go down the other road so I turn right on faith. I came to the angry road ... what does an angry road look like... couldn't really quite tell but then I came to the overpass of acceptance. I passed over the angry road toward home.

There was a very slippery road to my left ...the road of self-pity. A less traveled road ran alongside that pitiful road... it seemed to move upward... never seen a hill on the way home before ... how could I have missed it?

There was the misty road of doubt. I couldn't quite tell where it led ... so I took another road... there were frequent signs along this road, looking like ethereal Burma shave signs ... on each was written a promise from God. The view is so much clearer on that road of promise... There was a lonely road but then it seemed that I was surrounded with family, friends, and prayers.... there was a gentle shepherd leading the way.

I am home now... but not quite home. Loving wife, amazing family, friends like I have not had for many years... but not quite home. There's more road that lies ahead. Faith, love, acceptance, caring for others... but not exactly the thruway. It will be a slow road, sometimes achy, sometimes discouraging, but never alone, never without hope, never without a foundation that will not be moved.

*All very spiritual... this is what a Christian does... when he is bummed out... and things basically stink. This is what **this** Christian does... writes/preaches it until he believes and follows the road of faith ... thankful he doesn't have to do it alone.*

When challenged and overwhelmed by life we can choose the road of faith. We need not take the angry, misty, slippery roads. Our faith does not change with the circumstances of life; the foundation is solid. Our feelings and emotions easily deceive and mislead us. They fluctuate with the ups and downs of life and are not enough to bring us through the gale force realities of it. It is important to remind ourselves that the foundations of our faith cannot be shaken.

Live the Faith – Strengthen the Foundation

There is so much about life and death, fate and choice, joy and sorrow that is puzzling and unclear. We, along with the apostle Paul, see through a glass darkly. There are many things that cause us to ask why? Why me? Why them? Why now? It begins to feel like the super structure of our lives is coming apart. When the storms of life come our way, it is time to shore up the foundation of our faith.

We have friends who live right on the shore of beautiful Quincy Bay in Massachusetts. I have lived on the prairie and appreciate the beauty of the open sky. But growing up near the shore has left me with a love of the sounds and sights and beauty of the ocean. So if I Face the Facts – I am dealing with some less than noble feelings of envy.

When our friends bought the house, it was supported by 10-12 inch posts built into the incline leading down to the beach. The posts were worn and dangerously unstable; certainly unsafe standing against the harsh New England winters. They did not bring in a contractor to fix the problem in six easy weeks and 250 not so easy payments. Rather, over the years they dug around each post, building solid foundation stones around each one. It was a way of life, making sure the foundation was solid – they knew the storms were coming.

The time to build a solid faith foundation is *before* the storms. In the confused, questioning and doubting times our foundation needs to be firm. When there are many things that we cannot understand, it is vital that we know those things which are true and solid. It is important to know that in crisis, pain, unfairness, and maybe even cruelty, some things are absolutely and irrevocably true.

Review the foundation stones of faith:

God is Real

God is Love

God is at Work

Whatever the catastrophic, life shattering experiences that come our way – nothing need ever change the foundation of our faith – the truth is always truth. By nature, we are attuned to the order and beauty around us, and all have a basic, inner longing for truth; something deep within each of us knows that there *is* a God. In Christ we see the very character of God. We see Jesus, we see our heavenly Father who reveals himself in his Son. As we learn to trust and obey this God of love we see his grace at work and we know experientially that he is at work.

Our faith remains strong when built on the solid foundation of those things we know and believe are always true. In the crisis, we are tempted to forget that we really do believe that

God is Real … He is Love … He is at Work. When shaken by life we must shore up our foundations; reminding ourselves of that which we know for sure.

Live the Faith – Seek God

A solid faith, however, is more than just figuring things out. Faith is much deeper than merely knowing and believing that which is factual. We can be theologically correct, philosophically astute, logically sound yet also fearful, defeated and overwhelmed.

Dallas Willard in his book, *Hearing God*, speaks of what he calls "blind" faith:

> Here we find ourselves believing in God and believing that he is with us. Perhaps we believe because of past experiences or because we have faith in the faith of others, or even because of abstract reasoning that tells us he simply *must* be there …
>
> Although this kind of faith is not to be despised - far from it – the human heart must not be content to treat God's being with us as merely a matter of blind faith with nothing else to go on. Abstract reasoning from the doctrine of God's omnipresence, or mental assent to the dogma that God must be with the believer, faith in the faith of others, or even remembrances of past experiences of God – none of these can be an adequate foundation for sustained spiritual growth. *(Hearing God)*

And I would add that none of these – are an adequate source of strength and resolve when life shakes you up.

Often life is so ruthless that the mere recitation of a memorized catechism or a glibly read string of promises can leave us still weak, lost and fearful. There is more to faith than a theological understanding that God exists, that he cares for us and is at work for us. Faith is a very real, deeply intimate relationship with a personal God that grows even deeper and stronger in the storms of life. Oswald Chambers writes, "Until we can come face to face with the deepest, darkest fact of life, without changing our view of God's character, we do not yet know him." *(My Utmost for His Highest)*

***

John Wesley was a deeply earnest, well nigh unto obsessive, Anglican priest. His deepest desire was to be holy and obey God. As a young priest he made his way across the Atlantic Ocean to Georgia as a missionary to the Indians. Even as he sailed across the sea, he was preaching, teaching, praying and administering the sacraments to those on board. Every moment was devoted to seeking and serving God. In his journal he spoke of his daily schedule:

> We now began to be a **little** *(are you kidding me?)* regular. Our common way of living was this: - from four to five in the morning, each of us used private prayer. From five to seven we read the Bible together ... at seven we breakfasted. At eight we were the public prayers. From nine to twelve I usually learned German ... At twelve we met to give an account of one another what we had done

since our last meeting and what we designed to do before our next ... sic. *(Wesley's Journal)*

It goes on like that; lunch at 1pm, 2pm reading to the passengers, 4pm evening prayers, 5pm private prayer, 6pm more reading with some passengers, 7pm German service, 8pm another meeting to check up on one another, 9-10pm sleep. And this was on a cruise ship! This guy **really** had faith i.e. he really *believed* God.

But it wasn't long before the storm blew in and that obsessive compulsive religious cruise ship began to rock and roll! Wesley describes waves that ... "rose to the heavens above and clave to hell beneath." He was overwhelmed with fear and was ... "ashamed of my unwillingness to die." Asking himself, "How is it that thou art unwilling to die?" At the same time he observed the German Christians calmly singing a psalm through the entire storm.

All of Wesley's striving and seeking were inadequate as he faced the reality of life and death. Clearly, knowing and believing the right stuff was not enough when the storm threatened to turn his ship upside down. He confessed. "I have a fair summer religion. I can talk well; nay and believe myself, while no danger is near: But let death look me in the face and my spirit is troubled." *(Wesley's Journal)* Without a warm, genuine, intimate, life changing relationship with God, Wesley was unable to face the storms of life that broke in upon him.

In his search for God, Wesley speaks of going "very unwillingly" to a society on Aldersgate Street where at about quarter to nine he felt his "heart strangely warmed." He continues, "I **felt** I did trust in Christ, Christ alone for salvation: and an assurance was given me that he had taken away *my* sins, even *mine* and saved *me* from the law of sin and death."

It is vital to have a clear assurance of the unshakeable, immoveable foundation stones of faith. No matter what our feelings, whatever the situation, nothing will change that: God is Real (a reality) … God is Love (in character) … and God is at Work (through grace). But while a solid faith foundation is vital; a genuine, warm, personal relationship with God through his one and only Son Jesus Christ is indispensible. Living our faith is less about what we *believe* and more about what we *do* and how we respond in *relationship* with God.

While a solid faith foundation is vital; a genuine, warm, personal relationship with God through his one and only Son Jesus Christ is indispensible.

Our faith in God is more than a tool needed to smooth out the bumps of life. Faith is a deep confidence in God; its source being a very real, very personal relationship with him. This faith, this confidence, this relationship then becomes an inner source of never failing hope, guidance, stability, and confidence.

God is a God of revelation seeking to make himself known. In the harmony of nature, we see the nature of God. In Jesus Christ, we see God seeking to restore a relationship with us as his children. In the very beginning, we see God walking and talking with Adam and Eve in the Garden of Eden. The whole revelation of scripture is the account of God's pursuing and pleading that we (as his creation) would return to an intimate relationship with Him. The innate longing of our heart for God, is the sound of his voice within, calling us to come to him as his children. He is seeking to live in union with us in the joy, pain, triumphs, and defeats of life.

Now it gets pointedly personal. In a way, I would extend a literary altar call. I sort of believe in altar calls. (Sort of … because I have seen preachers in my formative years harangue and harass guilt ridden Christians to walk to the front of the church, as a validation of their oratory prowess.) I *believe* in altar calls, however, because when we hear God's calling us into a closer walk with him - it is good to respond.

Is your heart strangely warmed by the presence of God? The warmth of a genuine personal relationship with a benevolent God is your deepest need. A cold clinical faith system will not bring the strength and courage you need in the cataclysms of life. A sweet loving Jesus is adequate to get you by when they snicker at your born again profession at work or school.

But when the storms really start to shake, rattle, rock and roll your ship on the sea of life, you will need the very presence of the all mighty God of the universe. The good news of the gospel is that: "God was in Christ reconciling the world unto himself." In the crises of life – Live the Faith – stay close to God. Don't settle for calculating philosophy or cold religion. For in the crisis you need nothing less than the warmth of the presence of God himself.

Many view God as a task master and relate to him as one would to a building inspector. Some day he is going to inspect, (we think) ... so we scurry around making sure everything is proper and in its place. But there are so many regulations - it's sure we have missed several. "I hope he doesn't look too close. How am I doing now God? OK ... OK ... I know I need to work on those things ... let me try again." God was in Christ reconciling the world to himself, not enrolling us in his data base so he can document our non-compliance to an onerous list of regulatory divine legislation.

Facing the uncertain and fearful times of life in relationship with God *always* brings a greater closeness to him. Walking through the valley of the shadow of death or through the fiery blast with God reinforces our desperate need for him; peeling away the façade of adequacy and self effort. We are no longer trying to impress God but hanging on to him in a state of total reliance.

A personal relationship with God is just that ... personal. The fact remains that there are no ten easy steps with a money back guarantee of intimacy with God. Personal relationships do not happen "by the numbers." Inter-personal warmth and intimacy begins with an introduction and deepens within the context of shared life experiences. A personal relationship with God begins with reconciliation in Christ and is strengthened in the crucible of real life. The stress and strain of life can toughen the love of a husband and wife and strengthen the family. In the same way, facing the hard times of life, in close relationship with God can (and will) be a source of grace and peace.

In one sense, all of humanity has a relationship with God. The nature of the awareness of and closeness to God varies widely. Some, likely most, have a distant relationship with him. Others live in denial of the existence of God. Some, especially those in crisis, are angry with God. Others are just annoyed at his intrusion into their lives. Some are fearful of God's judgment while still others have a pleasant Pollyanna, "I'm OK – Your OK" relationship with the God of creation. The fact remains that we are created in the image of God so that we find our greatest strength, peace, and contentment in closeness to him.

"Our hearts are restless until they rest in thee, O Lord."

Augustine

"There is a God shaped vacuum in the heart of every man which cannot be filled by any created thing, but only by God, the Creator, made known through Jesus."

Blaise Pascal

How then do we live "in relationship" with God?

Live the Faith – Talk to God

There is nothing more important than the discipline of spending time alone with God. Time spent listening to a personal God and responding to him is the core of a relationship. In the time of crisis this time with God is even more important. Dallas Willard, in his book *Hearing God* speaks of this personal, intimate, closeness to God. "Today, I continue to believe that people are meant to live in an ongoing conversation with God, speaking and being spoken to."

Talking to God … all of a sudden we are talking about prayer – real, genuine, heartfelt prayer. Prayer brings a deepening closeness to God. In the times of trial and testing, our prayer life is no longer a mere religious obligation. As we lean upon God, we come to know him more fully as a God who truly does love us personally.

We know that prayer is not always easy. We are prone to the normal distractions of life; cars and kids, planes and trains, office work and yard work, Facebook and now Twitter. The pain and hurt of life becomes yet another annoying persistent distraction from closeness to God.

The turmoil in our lives can sap our resolve and cloud the reality of this personal and practical relationship with God. The unexpected difficulties of life demand our attention so forcibly that the priority of living close to God fades into the background. Here we are faced with another "on purpose" faith decision.

The crisis is not a distraction from prayer

but rather the occasion for prayer.

***

I have studied strategies of leadership and management quite extensively. One of the realities of any organization is that 20% of the people tend to do 80% of the work. In the church, 20% of the people provide 80% of the income. It is the 20% that teach Sunday school, work with the youth group, mow the lawn, and serve on the church board. As a pastor I have tried to improve that percentage to varying degrees of success.

The corollary to that 80% - 20% principal is that a pastor or manager tends to spend 80% of his or her time with those who are most demanding while at the same time contributing the least to the mission of the church. Pastors are not alone, however, for everyone knows that individual who is so self-absorbed and often so needy that they suck the life out of you and still want more.

These are important people, but there's only so much you can give in their care before time of rest and recovery is needed.

Parkinson's is an incurable disease. It is a disease that does not go away, very much like that needy demanding person that brings you to the point of exhaustion. I go to sleep unsettled with this demanding intruder; the randomness of its movements keeping me from sleep. The pins and needles, aches and pains keep me company in the middle of the night interrupting sleep. I wake up with it in the morning with its rustiness creaking in my bones. All day long, that bad breath salesman is there. He/she is very much one of those draining, demanding, and needy people that... with unrestricted access go wherever I go.

Think about that person who sits with you at lunch or corners you at church and your eyes glaze over as they go on and on ... their three favorite subjects ... me, myself and I. What if you went home... and there they were...locked the door to the bathroom and they're still there...open the door to the fridge and they want a snack. You can't even kick them out of bed! Hitchcock-esque to say the least.

The truly devastating and debilitating things of life are those things that do not go away. These things will either overwhelm and distract us from prayer or they will be the occasion and opportunity *for* prayer and a deepening conversational relationship with God.

Live the Faith – Listen to God

It was April of 1979; standing outside Anaheim stadium in California, shaking my head. I was taking a feeble first step toward understanding an indispensible life lesson that is crucial to marital harmony and even survival.

Women understand things better than men.

Grasping this concept is foundational to a long, mostly healthy, happy, and harmonious marriage. My wife Brenda and I were married in Winnipeg, Manitoba, Canada. We drove across the prairies to Calgary to catch a flight to L.A. It was a wonderful trip, staying in a $15 hotel and ate most of our meals at taco stands and ocean side sea food shops. Breakfast was served each day in our room; self serve, not room service. We called it romantic … my kids call it cheap.

One of the first things I checked upon arriving in California was the baseball schedule. Living in Saskatchewan, some 400 miles north of Montana, baseball was rarely on TV and going to a game was out of the question. I was more than excited to find out that the Angels were in town. I was positively ecstatic, as a Boston native, to see that they would be playing the Red Sox.

It was the very next day, I think, that we made our way down to the box office outside the stadium. My goal was to get the best seats possible, not knowing when this opportunity would come again. As I waited impatiently the line began to disperse and the word filtered back ... sold out! I was so disappointed, crest fallen, depressed, etc., etc.

Especially as a new bride, my wife was very much committed to her recent vows to love, honor, and pamper her husband till death do us part. Her positive, encouraging and cheery response was: "Let's wait awhile, maybe someone will give us tickets." She very much wanted to make me feel better but that's what got me shaking my head.

My first unexpressed thought; "what does my poor Canadian wife know about major league baseball?" Cities in the northeast, i.e. Boston and New York, have a rather vain and at times even pompous view of themselves. I now live in New York and we speak of "the city" i.e. New York, as though no other city exists. Bostonians refer to Boston as the Hub, as in the hub of the universe. It is likely that four years of living in Kansas City and four years of living in Canada, had not quite freed me fully from all of that pomposity. So even though I still loved my new bride very much, it was obvious that she was a rube from Canada needing enlightenment.

Still shaking my head, I responded quickly, "People do NOT just give away tickets to an Angels/ Red Sox game!" Her reaction was just a semi-smug knowing look and now my head is really shaking. It was no more than 30 seconds later, a gentleman approached us; "I have two box seat tickets I don't need, would you like them?"

(Are you kidding me?!) As we make our way to our seats, my head is lowered, but still shaking. We were three rows up from the third base line, you could hear the base coach and players ... best seats I ever had.

In over thirty years of marriage, we have never said "I told you so", even once. But I think, even now, there is a touch of smugness when my wife thinks back to that day. And a touch of that "humility-put in my place" feeling may still linger in my psyche, as I learned one of the most important principles of marital bliss:

Women understand things better than men!

There is more than a little hesitation in the comparison of my wife's blind luck to the infinite wisdom of God. But when we are overwhelmed with life, we need to listen to one who knows all things far better than we do. Foundational to the Christian faith is the conviction that the Bible is the word of God. This is perhaps the greatest leap of faith as we seek a relationship with God. Our faith as a follower of Christ rises or falls on the authenticity, integrity, and trustworthiness of scripture. Countless men and women over three millennia bear witness that the Biblical revelation has been to them the very voice of God.

The good news, especially in those "life shakes you up" times, is that the help, strength, wisdom and comfort of God's words addressed to you will become more real than they ever have before. When shaken by life, the scripture becomes our crisis response manual.

To some the Bible is a dry old dusty book; irrelevant to our day. To others the Bible is a collection of literature to be appreciated academically. Still others accept the Bible as divine revelation among other sacred writings. There are as well those who treat the Bible as a magic book, which will solve every problem and heal all disease if only the right verse is applied. For those of us shaken by life, the Bible is an invaluable personal practical guide as we endeavor to live out our faith. The Bible is the record of 3,000 years of men and women seeking and finding God. In the Bible is found the real stuff of life; the good, the bad, and the ugly. Any situation: whether it is pain, death, murder, incest, doubt or fear is addressed in the Bible, which we accept by faith as God's personal love letter to his children.

The Bible brings a faith perspective into our lives. I have mentioned several times how easy it is to be overwhelmed with the devastation of life, that all we can see is the pain and suffering. The scripture, as God's words, help us step back and see the whole picture. His speaking to us reminds us of the unshakeable foundation stones of faith: God is Real ... God is Love ... God is at Work.

Face the Facts ... Accept the Feelings ... Count the Blessings ... Live the Faith ... Trust the future to God is such good advice (– and mostly functional as chapter titles.) But they are so much easier written and quoted than lived out in real life. The Bible can teach us and encourage us as we respond to crisis with faith. It is an instruction manual for all of life. But if there is one book that is specifically helpful for spiritual crisis management; it would be the Psalms. The Psalms are full of the joy, pain, celebration, doubt, fear, and failures of people in crisis as they call out to God.

Read the Psalms relationally i.e. as a means of growing closer to God. Note how they help, encourage, and guide the reader to an intentional faith response. The songs of Israel are unashamedly intimate with God. Again and again the psalmist cries out:

"Why do the nations conspire and the peoples plot in vain?" (*Psalm 2:1*)

"Why, O LORD, do you stand far off? Why do you hide yourself in times of trouble?" (*Psalm 10:1*)

"I say to God my Rock, Why have you forgotten me? Why must I go about mourning, oppressed by the enemy?" (*Psalm 42:9*)

"Why O Lord do you reject me and hide your face from me?" (*Psalm 88:14*)

Yet at the same time the Psalms are filled with praise and rejoicing:

"The LORD is my strength and my shield; my heart trusts in him, and I am helped. My heart leaps for joy and I will give thanks to him in song." *(Psalms 28:7)*

"Enter his gates with thanksgiving and his courts with praise; give thanks to him and praise his name." *(Psalm 100:4)*

"Praise the LORD. Give thanks to the LORD, for he is good; his love endures forever." *(Psalms 106:1)*

Words of hope, spoken by a loving God become seeds of hopefulness even when we face the trouble and trauma of life:

"Guide me in your truth and teach me, for you are God my Savior, and my hope is in you all day long." *(Psalms 25:5)*

"Be strong and take heart, all you who hope in the LORD." *(Psalms 31:24)*

"Why are you downcast, O my soul? Why so disturbed within me? Put your hope in God, for I will yet praise him, my Savior and my God." *(Psalms 43:5)*

The time of crisis and distress is the time to find practical help and needed strength in the scripture. It is crucial to recognize that God speaks to us in a personal way through his word. As we live our faith, seeking God, and talking to God, we are wise to listen to God's words as well. It is great wisdom to grow close to a

loving personal God ... A God who is Real... A God who is
Loving ... A God who is at Work.

Live the Faith - Share in Community

Bill and Diane were good friends. They had been a part of
the church fellowship for several years, working with kids, men's
ministry, and the softball team. Bill especially was unashamed and
positive in speaking to others of his faith. He was someone all the
kids loved, mainly because he loved them, but his generosity in
sharing his candy didn't hurt his popularity either.

Bill and Diane had always wanted to have children. They
prayed and waited ... waited and prayed and finally received the
good news; Diane was pregnant! All of their family members,
church friends and neighbors shared in the joy and anticipation of
the coming birth. They praised God for answering their prayers.

(You can guess where this story is going.) Unfortunately
after three months, Diane had a miscarriage. Understandably, they
were devastated ... overwhelmed with the loss. How could God
play with their emotions in this way? Why would he give them
such hopes only to shatter them so cruelly? They were angry with
God; no longer on speaking terms. The tsunami of sorrow and loss
seemed to sweep away their faith and shatter their relationship
with God. Bill and Diane never again came to church or shared in
fellowship with those who loved them. They divorced themselves

from the church, turning away from the healing grace of a loving and personal God. Henry Nouwen writes:

> Much of our isolation is self-chosen. We do not like to be dependent on others and, whenever possible, we try to show ourselves that we are in control of the situation and can make our own decisions. This self-reliance has many attractions. It gives us a sense of power, it allows us to move quickly, it offers us the satisfaction of being our own boss, and it promises many rewards and prizes. However, the underside of self-reliance is loneliness, isolation, and the constant fear of not making it in life. (*Here and Now*)

When life crashes in around us, the temptation is to withdraw from fellowship. How can we face people when we ache so badly inside? How can we worship when God seems so distant? The fact remains that in the time of crisis the answer is not withdrawal. A very large part of the needed help and healing comes within a faith community where there is love and care.

Live the Faith - Worship God

I come from an evangelical, biblically conservative, faith community. There is a strong emphasis on an intimate relationship with a loving, personal God. The emphasis on the personal can at times, however, take away from the sacramental nature of the Church of Christ. It is important to understand that God is present in the gatherings and workings of the church.

The worship gatherings of a faith community are sacramental. It is within the context of worship that God speaks words of wisdom, breathes new hope into our spirit, and opens our eyes to the hopefulness of living in union with him. The testimony of the Church is that God's working in this way is unexplainable – but undeniable. The experience of God's presence in worship brings healing, new resolve, conviction, freedom and touches the heart on a spiritual level far more effectively than any structured spiritual growth or maturity program.

The time of crisis and pain is not the time to avoid worship. There are times when the trauma is so great or the struggle so overwhelming it is even hard to pray. But worship in times of weakness and dependence can be the most genuine worship of all. Certainly seeking God in a time of need is more significant than the normal everyday routine tends to be. All too common is the pattern of rushing into the sanctuary five minutes late with coffee on the breath; enjoy the hymns, doze through prayer and tell the pastor "good sermon" at the end. (We pastors appreciate the "good sermon" gesture as we shake you out of the church. In fact, according to my parishioners/friends, I never preached a bad sermon. It is likely why we pastors all think we are great preachers.) In times of need, our approach to God is that of brokenness and humility. David wrote: "The sacrifices of God are a broken and contrite heart." *(Psalms 51; 17a)* Participation in worship draws on the faith and prayers of those who worship along side of you. The hymns of praise, in a sense are praise for you. In the pastoral prayer you are interceded for. The sacraments, the Eucharist, are a means of grace as we share an intimacy with God that can only be described as communion ... communion with God.

Live the Faith – Acceptance not Submission

My resignation from ministry as a pastor was perhaps the greatest struggle I faced. Facing new limitations was and is the source of my greatest frustration and even at times anger. The greatest casualty of Parkinson's disease is the theft of *my* ministry, *my* life's work, and the excitement of looking forward to 20 years or so of *my* ministry as a pastor.

Standing back, taking a look at my angst, it is not too difficult to see a somewhat less than faith-full response. There are far too many personal pronouns in this response to reflect a solid faith that God is Real ... God is Love ... and God is at Work. The work ethic was ingrained into the person and pastor I had become.

As a pastor of 25+ years, I had a pretty good sense of what it meant to live my faith. I knew that my first priority was to spend time with God, so I wouldn't be too cranky with the people, and so I would have the resources I need to serve others. I knew that I must pray much and plan well to see progress or success in ministry. I knew unless I built leaders and included people in praying and planning there would be no shared vision. I knew that I was not a mega church pastor. Writing these words, they seem rather presumptuous in an "I've got it all figured out" kind of way. But I've got that covered too because I *knew* that I didn't have it all figured out. At times I still wonder what shape my ministry would have taken had I not been diagnosed with Parkinson's disease. My best bet is that I would have become much more, or at least somewhat more, radical in the "last ten years/nothing to lose" period of my ministry. Maybe God was trying to save his kingdom from the fallout of that scenario.

There was great struggle as I tried to get a handle on what it meant to live out my faith while facing the annoyance and restriction of disease. I am old enough to be old school. Pastoral candidates were indoctrinated with the idea that a pastor must work hard. A "successful" pastor (i.e. lots of bodies and maybe even souls in the pews) shared his secret of success with a few of us young pastors. "There are only three things you need to do to be successful in ministry" he said … "Work! Work! Work!" The generation before me was called to pastoral ministry within the context of a holiness revival. My generation was called to pastoral ministry in the context of the revival of the Jesus people. We didn't fit the mold. In fact we hated anything that faintly resembled any kind of mold.

Everything was changing. Dress codes were out the window. Suddenly rock and roll and Jesus were being used in the same sentence. The 60's era was a rebellion against hypocrisy, materialism, war, and violence. The jargon of the day was "do your own thing, don't trust anyone over 30, make love not war, and give peace a chance." There was a throng of young people who became genuine followers of Christ. These Jesus people were out to change the world for Jesus.

I was part of this vast group of Jesus people who would go out into our world gossiping about Jesus. Jesus' commandment to go into the world with the good news was a life style. College campuses, spring break, coffee houses, rock and roll concerts, were all vehicles for the good news of the gospel. To a certain extent, however, we (as in old hippy types), inherited the standards of the greatest generation, those of the WWII era. The expectations of a pastor were quite clear: a minimum 60 hour work week, knock on doors, have lots of kids in Sunday school, make at least 1,000 calls (i.e. homes visits) each year, and incidentally preach twice on Sunday, teach Wednesday, and lead youth group Friday nights. It was an all consuming life, and not without biblical precedent. Paul spoke of pouring out his life as a drink offering and of sharing his very life as well as the gospel.

As a young pastor, I did everything in the church not the least of which was the weekly bulletin. The process began with a paraffin stencil upon which letters would be typed. This stencil was cut in half, unless there was the good fortune of having a wide carriage type writer. The announcements, statistics, order of service, and information were typed on the stencil; if a mistake was made it could be corrected with some ether smelling red liquid stuff. These fumes were pretty strong; overuse could be hazardous. There were even reports of some rather fantastic, pseudo-spiritual visions among pastors who were overly prone to typos in need of correction.

The art work was then added. These cute little pictures of everything from picnic baskets, to flags and banner headings came on a blue sheet that was inserted in the bulletin. The item would be cut off the blue page, traced on the white wax stencil, the shape cut out of the stencil and the little picture glued in. THEN, the two previously cut halves were glued together. THEN the full stencil was placed on the mimeograph machine, saturated with ink and printed on the bulletin paper. A blotter page went between each bulletin as it cranked out of the machine. Upon drying, the bulletins were folded and ready for another Lord's Day. Seriously, we did that every week.

Workaholism was the name of the game. There is a central core of that which is positive in this legacy. It is a good thing to recognize that pastoral ministry is not just playing games. The ministry was and is joyful, fulfilling, and positive in so many ways. However, the nature of this life and calling is to be all consuming. Evangelism was the number one priority. Nothing was more important than bringing people to faith in Christ.

In the months following my diagnosis, this workaholic lifestyle had become, to quote my neurologist, "untenable." I could no longer work hard all week. Parkinson's was an adversary setting boundaries of weariness, stiffness, and confusion around me. I struggled with the affliction of PD and the false guilt of doing so much less than I still expected of myself.

When the tragic circumstances shake your identity and clamp limitations on what you are able to do, the most difficult faith decision of all is to accept that which has come our way. Henri Nouwen speaks of drinking our cup ... choosing our lives:

> Drinking our cup of life makes us own everything we are living. It is saying, "This is my life," but also "I want this to be my life." Drinking the cup of life is fully appropriating and internalizing our own existence, with all its sorrows and joys.
>
> It is not easy to do this. For a long time we might not feel capable of accepting our own life. We can move beyond our protest, put the cup of our life to our lips and drink it, slowly, carefully, but fully. *(Here and Now)*

Accepting the tragedy and pain of life is a daunting spiritual challenge. Living out our faith does not mean surrendering to the tragedy and pain of life, but to live with a sense of acceptance, not surrender. If we can somehow, with God, and by grace, live through our trial with faith - God will be glorified, people will be encouraged, and we will know the joy of the Lord as our strength.

I know experientially that living out our faith when devastated by life is not neat, and always includes much failure and inadequacy. Making a faith decision is not a once and done task in the life of the Christian. Making faith decisions is of necessity a way of life. Again and again we will need God's grace and presence to face the hard facts of life. Time after time we will need the comfort of God's spirit when we are frightened, depressed, or angry.

Counting our Blessings, Living our Faith in obedience, and Trusting the past, present and future will entail a daily decision. But with varying degrees of success and failure; we have a faith that is solid, a God who is love, and a future that is eternally secure.

5

Trust the Future to God

"The Lord your God will be with you wherever you go . . ."

More Than a Clunker

God really does take care of those who follow Him. We
are after all, kids of God's kingdom and to quote one popular
television preacher/pseudo theologian "God don't want us driving
no junk." Being a retired pastor on disability is not the most
lucrative endeavor. Keeping up with medical expenses, a monthly
mortgage and putting kids through college on a fixed income is a
significant challenge. One luxury we do enjoy, however, is our
shiny black Lincoln Continental. We enjoy the V8 power, recline
in the plush leather seats, and relax in air conditioned comfort as
we drive on the air soft suspension.

The fact that our Lincoln is fifteen years old does not take
away from any of the comfort we enjoy. We are genuinely
thankful for our automobile. It strikes me how much more we can

appreciate and enjoy material things as followers of Christ. As I write this, there are many of the top executives from the most prestigious firms in the nation jetting their way to Washington, DC to beg for money so that their firms will survive. There is no doubt in my mind that we enjoy our fifteen year old car many times more than any of those ultra-rich, mega-powerful executives in their faster than sound private jets. So already the Lincoln in the driveway is more than an old clunker.

It was sad news when my wife called with the report of a suicidal deer that had tragically chosen to take his final fatal leap in front of our big black Lincoln. The bumper was damaged, the grill cracked, the full light assembly was damaged, the fiber glass hood and fender were both cracked. There were no injuries aside from the poor troubled deer, but immediately "Cash for Clunkers" ran through my mind. "Cash for Clunkers" was a recent federal program to stimulate the viability of our automobile industry. The plan basically provided a tax credit of several hundred dollars for anyone who would buy a new car while scrapping their old gas guzzler. Sadly, our particular vehicle did not qualify, so we began to consider repair.

I began checking online for salvage parts, looked up the number of a friend who helped with a previous accident, trying to figure out what we could or should do. The parts; even from a salvage yard would be well over $1,000 plus shipping. The new parts would need to be painted, etc. It was looking like clunker heaven for our black, shiny, favorite car. The situation was obviously in God's hands, and we lived with the confidence that he would provide for his children.

My Parkinson's diagnosis came with very real financial consequences. We were looking at fifteen to twenty years of previously expected income, that would now not come in. But God has his ways of provision. Somehow we live in a beautiful, small house of our own, have put four children through college, and we eat three or four meals almost every day. So we knew that God does indeed work. We prayed for his direction.

A couple days later there was a knock on my door (guess he couldn't figure out how to put the two wires together to ring the door bell ... got to fix that door bell). Looking out the front window, I could see another 1995 black shiny Lincoln in my driveway. A man was at the door telling me that he was getting rid of his 1995 black Lincoln Continental and wanted to know if I would buy his tires. I looked his car over and told him that I didn't really need tires but I could put the rest of his car to good use. Well, his car was going to be federally clunked on Saturday and it was then Thursday night.

I called my good friend John who is a mechanic / carpenter / handy man / do most anything kind of guy. (This is the same John who had been battling cancer for the past year and a half. He had a debilitating chemotherapy treatment a few days before, but said he would be glad to help.) Tony is the father of a handicapped child that my wife cares for as a nurse, who *just happened* to have a full shop with a lift and everything needed to do the work. Tony *just happened* to have the day off and was willing to help.

The next day John and I drove two Lincolns over to Tony's house to swap the damaged parts for those providentially salvaged from the soon to be cashed in clunker. The next six hours we extracted and replaced hundreds of screws, clips, belts, and apart from a somewhat crumpled front door, our well beloved luxury car looked new again.

There was much more that happened during those six hours. How inspiring it was that John shared with Tony, very easily as one friend to another, how the love and strength from God had made the last year and a half the best months of his life. There was a bonding that happened as three men were blessed to be part of God's working.

I don't fully understand the workings of God's providence. Does God hunt deer with Lincoln Continentals? Does He always deliver car parts? Is every stubbed toe an act of God? When I think too much about it my brain starts to hurt. There is much about the workings of God's providence that is beyond my understanding. There are, however, some things I do know ... or maybe more accurately ...there are some things I "faith". I know that God was at work in all these things for good. My wife and I look ahead to an uncertain future dealing with Parkinson's disease. What a beautiful re-assurance that God's "eye" is upon us. Or more importantly that because of God's grace we can live in relationship with the God of the universe and have the resources of his strength and the guidance of his wisdom. We are stronger in the faith that He will continue to work for our good.

A good Catholic man followed God's voice leading him to knock on a stranger's door to deliver his car parts. He was excited as well that his shiny black Lincoln could be an organ donor before the fatal clunking at the dealership. My friend John, who was so close to heaven, had another opportunity to splash joy and peace all over a new friend's driveway as we worked. Tony was more than a bit splashed on. The God of creation has received honor and glory as the story is retold of a special delivery from God's Salvage Yard Inc.

We believe in a God who provides. God is a personal God; a God who cares. And my wife and I really do enjoy our house in the New York suburbs, with a beautiful garden, swimming pool, and even a hot tub. If only it were that simple.

***

Battle Plan from the General

Joshua found out that trusting God with the future of his people did not rule out great pain and bloodshed. I'm not so sure my fun and inspiring Lincoln story would do the battle scarred Joshua much good. My newly repaired Lincoln was a clear answer to prayer. But Joshua was really up against it.

Joshua was marching across the Jordan River, into the Promised Land. Marching across the Jordan River on dry ground was a declaration of war on the inhabitants. He would be facing bloodshed, brutality, fear and loss. This was no Sunday school picnic - this was the real deal. Life and death decisions were placed squarely on his shoulders. He would watch his fellow Israelites fighting for their lives, arms hacked off, throats cut, and decapitations... well you get the idea.

What was Joshua's response, as he faced a life-and-death struggle? How would he respond in his time of crisis? God spoke clearly to Joshua with words of promise, hope, courage, and direction. Joshua went forward with optimism and courage with God's promise.

> No one will be able to stand up against you all the days of your life. As I was with Moses, so I will be with you; I will never leave you nor forsake you. Be strong and very courageous. Be careful to obey all the law my servant Moses gave you; do not turn from it to the right or to the left, that you may be successful wherever you go. Do not let this Book of the Law depart from your mouth; meditate on it day and night, so that you may be careful to do everything written in it. Then you will be prosperous and successful. (*Joshua 1:5, 7-8*)

The voice of God reminded Joshua of the past. Joshua was presented with an opportunity to reinforce the foundation of his faith. Looking back, he could see the workings of God in an unmistakable way; timid stuttering Moses standing before the great

Pharaoh… The Red Sea parting as he and his family passed safely through… The manna in the desert… The Ten Commandments hand delivered from the top of Mount Sinai.

As Joshua would look back at the ways that God had indeed been with Moses, he would reinforce the reality that, God is…Real. He had experienced that God is… Love. He had seen with his own eyes that God is… at Work. Joshua could still go forward: knowing the foundation of his faith was not shaken.

God was with Joshua, and with the people of Israel. They did have pain. They did have suffering. There was horrific bloodshed. But they did win the victory. The walls of Jericho did come tumbling down; they entered into the land of God's promise. Joshua found out that trusting God really did lead to triumph and conquest. So we understand that every life includes a certain amount, sometimes an unexplainable measure, of pain, suffering, and injustice. The faith and leadership of Joshua is an inspiring story. There was suffering, but the good guys won and God's people were settled in the Promised Land. There are times, however, when pain and suffering seem to come without a final vindication of victory and triumph.

The Good Guys Don't Always Win

Bill Betranger is a name few would recognize. At 35 Bill Betranger was one of the youngest Superior Court judges in Indiana state history. He was young, aggressive, idealistic and inflexible. He was known as the "hanging judge." Shortly after his election to his judicial position, to everyone's surprise, and even to his own surprise, Judge Betranger became a Christian. He was still strongly principled but began to look at the law in a different way.

Fred Palmer was a rather pathetic case. He had broken into a newlyweds' house while they were on their honeymoon and stolen all their wedding presents. His prior offenses, Charles Colson in his book, *Loving God* writes…"included marijuana possession, auto theft, possession of stolen property, but all except one of public drunkenness were committed after returning service in Vietnam. His service record was also noted: Bronze Star, National Defense Ribbon, Air Medal, Vietnam Service Medal, Vietnam Campaign Medal, and honorable discharge." *(Loving God)* Palmer, as well, had a wife and one-year-old daughter.

Judge Betranger was about to render a decision that would change his life and the life of Fred Palmer forever. Under the existing code, the charges against this young Armed Forces veteran carried a mandatory ten to twenty year sentence. The family and friends of the newlyweds who were burglarized were in attendance calling for the maximum to be applied to this case. However, Indiana lawmakers had passed new legislation providing more flexibility in sentencing for this type of crime. This new code, unfortunately for the Palmer family, would not come into effect until eighteen days after his arrest.

As Judge Betranger pronounced sentence, he determined that ruining the life of a young father by sentencing him to decades behind bars would be an invective, cruel and unusual punishment - against the Indiana state constitution. He then ruled in the interest of society, as well as the Palmer family that he served one year, minus the 160 days already served, followed by five years probation.

Fred Palmer served his time, studied his Bible, was involved with Prison Fellowship, and grew as a Christian. Fred was released after seven months, reunited with his family, and approached the victims of his crimes to begin to pay restitution. God was rewarding his faithfulness. Judge Betranger also was growing as a Christian and became more involved in his local church.

A year following Palmer's release the judge received notice of the Supreme Court's decision regarding his sentencing procedure. It was determined that the sentence was improperly applied and that Fred Palmer must return to prison to finish his sentence of ten to twenty years. Included in the decision was an indictment of Judge Betranger for contempt of court.

Fred Palmer was returned to prison to serve twenty more months until he was released on special clemency of the governor. And now the judge was facing his own legal action. Bill Betranger's life was never the same. His reputation was ruined, and rather than fight the indictment he chose to resign from his position, after which the Supreme Court dropped the charges. At the time of Colson's publishing the account of this courageous judge, he was operating a struggling law practice from a small house in Elkhart, Indiana. He reported business as scarce and said that reporters didn't come around anymore. They moved on to other stories.

As a result, few people have heard of the courageous, young judge with promising political aspirations, who was ready to stand against the world. In one sense, he has never equaled his previous influence and has wondered himself whether he made much of any impact. It is clear that Bill Beltranger Faced the Facts – Accepted the Feelings – he probably tried to Count his Blessings – Lived His Faith – and definitely had to Trust His Future to God. But he lost his job. He lost his reputation. And I doubt that God delivered car parts to his door.

Colson concludes that "obedience to God does not always mean a happy ending." Then Colson asked the question, "But why should we think it would?" To trust in God and obey his ways does not guarantee my cure for Parkinson's disease. And whatever our situation, or lot in life, the struggles we face, the injustices we endure, the diagnoses we think we don't "deserve" are the product of some combination of God's providence, our strengths and weaknesses, personal decision, and a certain amount of randomness in a "rain falls on the just and the unjust" kind of way.

But in all of this, the foundations of faith remain strong

and immovable. God is Real ... God is Love ... God is at Work. We don't see all that he's doing neither do we understand the totality of the infinity of his wisdom and working. And so if we are unemployed... God still is Real. If we are mistreated... God is still Love; he does not change. If I am a Parkinson's patient for the rest of my life, I still know this God – whose love is revealed through Jesus Christ – is still at Work. In pain, suffering, and injustice I can still Trust my Future to him.

So even if God is with us, life does not come with guarantees against that which is seemingly tragic in life. On one level there is always some silver lining around that which is most evil and demonic. But the thin etching of silver around the global unbridled evil of the Holocaust is barely evident. It hardly seems worth it. Sometimes the good guys just don't seem to win. At the same time it is neither necessary, nor wise, and certainly not a faith response, to live out all the worst-case scenarios of life. As people of faith we need to make intentional decisions to live each day by faith and not without all the "what-ifs" of life.

"What-ifs"

Parkinson's disease is incurable, progressive and debilitating. The resulting "what-ifs" clamor for my attention on a regular basis.

It was a beautiful day in the neighborhood. The sun was shining, the sky was blue, a few clouds in the sky and no breeze; a great day to be alive. This was a day perfect for golf; a game I have enjoyed since being a 12-year-old caddie at New Bedford, MA Country Club. The game has been especially fulfilling for me in these past years since I stopped keeping score.

However, instead of golfing, I was attending a symposium on Parkinson's disease. My wife and I found a parking spot on the beautiful collegial campus of Vassar College in Poughkeepsie, New York. This was shortly after my diagnosis; and I was in full education/information gathering mode. It was not long before I reached information overload in the education process. But at this point I wanted to learn all I could. The symposium would last most of the day with doctors, surgeons, neurologists, social workers, and psychologists all having their say. This was a very helpful and informative time. It was good for me to understand and just as important for my wife to understand some of the challenges that lay before us. The information was helpful; personally however, I found the setting less than encouraging.

These people were old! What was I doing in a room full of over 300 old, shaking, drooling senior citizens. This is not part of the plan. My plan was to be sixty years and old playing basketball with the kids. I anticipated being one of those old guys who would cheat, hold, and annoy the youngsters who would want to play a real game of basketball. Shuffling gait, slurred speech and progressing dementia were not something I intentionally signed up for.

As I looked around, I began to wonder how long it would be before I was shuffling around with a walker. I watched these Parkinson's patients at lunch in their attempts to eat. The caregivers, mostly wives, would caringly wipe the drool from their spouses chin. It was quite touching, but I didn't want to be looking down the road toward that destination. As I began to walk down the chilling road of the "what-ifs" of the future the way became more and more slippery and dangerous. Staying on that road was going to bring me to convalescence by the end of the day.

Part of trusting God with the future is a refusal to live the "what-ifs" as though they were real. Looking at life through the lens of "what-if" brings fear, doubt, and insecurity. You see, the "what-if" lens is a zoom lens. The trials and challenges that lie ahead become larger and larger until they dominate our thoughts and plans. We need to understand that the painful realities of the future are seldom as large or as terrible as the anticipation.

***

It was 1963, and the what-ifs of my young life nearly did me in. The phone rang, I overheard my mother speaking to my younger brother, "Don't worry you'll be okay. I'll send Ken down to get you." My younger brother was at the YMCA, about eight or ten blocks from our home in New Bedford, Massachusetts. It sounded like he needed help.

Apparently he was trapped inside the YMCA building, because there was this tough guy standing outside ready to beat him up. I was twelve or thirteen at the time, so I was sent to rescue my brother. A couple of blocks from home and I began to question, "Why am I being sent on this perilous mission?" I didn't crack the 5 foot barrier until the sophomore year of high school, so I did not present much of an imposing figure. My brother was 6 foot 2 and three years older, surely he could handle the situation much better.

New Bedford was and I think is still a pretty tough town. Fights and challenges were a daily part of the school day. My particular life challenge of breaking the 5 foot barrier made it relatively easy to fly below the radar in my junior high school. Obviously, very few were looking to add a 4 foot 10 inch seventh grader to their list of conquests. So I was certainly not the man for the job.

As I got closer, the adversary I was about to face became bigger, uglier, meaner and scarier by the minute. Halfway there he was the meanest kid at school. Another block and he was the toughest guy in the high school. By the time I was a block away he was 300 pounds, covered with tattoos and just released on parole. I was frantically plotting and planning ways to sneak my brother out the back door of that YMCA.

As I arrived I slowly looked around the corner to the front entrance of the Y. A high-pitched voice was cursing, threatening, and creating significant verbal havoc. The good news is that this pseudo-scary would-be assailant was maybe 4 foot 6 inches, and all of 72 pounds. My day was made as I gallantly escorted my younger brother home to our very cool, 100-year-old sea captain's house on 62 State Street.

Looking toward the future through the fearful lens of the "what-ifs" will magnify the coming cataclysms *far* out of proportion. The storms are never (almost never) as devastating as the anticipation. The people are never (almost never) as mean as you fear. The news is never (almost never) as negative as you read. So don't live the "what-ifs" of life. Living out the "what ifs" of the future is not a response of faith.

"If-onlies"

In the same way it is mistake to live out the "if-onlies" of circumstances or regret. I shouldn't listen to the bad breath salesman anymore. His pitch is a lot like the bad infomercials that turn your head even when you know better. If only I had that golf club; I would take 10 strokes off my game. If only I use that magical cream; I would look 20 years younger. If only I had the slashing, chopping, dicing knife, my life in the kitchen would be a dream. If only I didn't have my disability I could really do what I want to do. If only you had not made that decision my life would be so much better.

My denial mechanisms for the most part have functioned well enough to insulate me from most of the "what-ifs" of life. I am more of a sucker for the salesman's pitch of the "if-onlies" that come to mind as part of coping with a progressing disability. Most of these come in the form of – "if only I didn't have this disability" - if only I could – but can't now.

The application process for receiving Social Security disability benefits is impersonal, demeaning, and often adversarial. I have always felt fairly competent in responding to aggressive people. More and more this is less and less the case. A Journal entry records my feeble attempts in response to the questionings at the Social Security medical exam.

November 17, 2004

> *I really am disabled. Believe me. I have a file full of documentation of my friends, colleagues, doctors trying to convince the governmental hierarchy that I can't do my job. So here I am in this cold institutional holding pen, with bulletproof glass protecting what look like prison nurses, the next step in my new career... disability.*

> *I greeted the receptionist in a pleasant and semi-humorous way, receiving a blank stare/annoyed look in return. There was a bulletproof kryptonite Plexiglas shield protecting the workers from the public. I couldn't find the opening through which to pass my paperwork so I*

was looking up and down and all-around with my
government form, in a bemusing kind of way. Sure it was
bemusing ... except that I thought the nurse was going to
call security... totally disgusted... someone should've told
her. The message of her menacing look was clear; "this is
serious business."

A nurse came out the side door with a look that
said, "Come with me peacefully and I won't have to use the
cuffs." As I entered her room/lair the door closed behind
me. We sat down, and looking back I know it was
intentional that her stool was 6 inches above my chair.
Looking down she barked, "Take your medicine out of the
bag." When do you take them? I struggled for words.
What did I feel like? UGH ... I got it wrong... a disgusted
look from the nurse. Now it is definitely time for
condescension. I sit up, drawing on all my educational
superiority and ministerial presence speaking distinctly in
a "listen closely dear I will speak English more clearly this
time and this time you need to get it right" tone of voice.
UGH... I gave the right time for the wrong medication.
She conquered me with another disgusted look. I must be
disabled. I can't even do condescension. And this nurse
desperately needed condescension.

She treated me as though I was no better than the
rest of the huddled masses in the cold welfare-esque office;

*she marched off in victory, the Nurse Ratchet of
Poughkeepsie. Routine doctors exam. The doctor came
in, took my vitals and signed her name with what I thought
was a sidelong look that said "you look fine to me." Now I
am wondering if I might need to spend another few months
convincing people of my disability.*

I still struggle with the "if-onlies" as in if only I could do
what I once was able to do. It is troubling to me that the burden of
family finances now falls on my wife. This past week I was
researching a car lease. Suddenly it struck me that I was no longer
capable of dealing with the details and discussing various options
with car salespeople. I still deal with anger when the long-term
diagnosis of Parkinsonian dementia is slowly and progressively
confirmed. I walked into the wrong bank and didn't even know it
was the wrong bank. I don't trust myself driving more than half an
hour – and this scares my wife to death. I don't like forgetting my
zip code or trying to figure how to set the table; which is one of the
things I should be able to handle. I don't like seeing a psychologist
shake his head a bit when I get stuck on fourth grade math
problems. I have one adorable lively redheaded granddaughter;
who is more fun than should be legal, and I naturally want to
impress her. The thought crossed my mind that I would like my
grandchildren to remember when their grandfather was not
demented, so I'm taking lots of video of myself being as cool
possible. The most common response from others about my
impending dementia is "Don't worry; I'm the same way even

worse." I can take that response for what it is, an attempt at reassurance, but I know it's not the same as the dementia I feel.

Can you see where the "if-onlies" can take us? Following this pathway of "if-onlies" will lead to self-pity, self absorption, and bitterness. Living from the perspective of if only I could do what I once could do or if only I could do what others can do will blind us to the blessings of God all around us and the resources of his grace. So trusting God with the future begins with trusting God with our present realities.

One Day at a Time

"One day at a time - sweet Jesus that's all I'm asking of you..." (Kristofferson/Wilkins 1974) croons the country Western song. In 1988 Bobby McFerrin reminded us, "Don't worry, be happy." The hackneyed response of every professional athlete when asked by an interviewer if his team can win the championship is: "Well Ned, we will just keep playing one game at a time." Those who have been helped by Alcoholics Anonymous live by the slogans; "take it easy" and "one day at a time." Dale Carnegie teaches that 90% of what you worry about never happens... and 90% of that is not as bad as you thought it would be. Calvin Coolidge said, "If you see ten troubles coming down the road, you can be sure that nine will run into the ditch before they reach you."

"One day at a time" is part of the very fabric of our world and societal consciousness. The secular humanist, evangelical fundamentalist, devout Muslim, and practitioners of Eastern religions all teach, in one way or another, the principal: "live one day at a time." We all understand the wisdom of living this way. Every one of us understands as well, how much easier it is to nod knowingly than to face our challenges, "one day at a time."

Jesus said:

"Therefore do not worry about tomorrow, for tomorrow will worry about itself. Each day has enough trouble of its own." (*Matthew 6:34)*

Jesus was probably not the first one to say "one day at a time" but he brought it up a long time before Dale Carnegie. Each day has enough trouble of its own… This means each day will have some trouble. Some days will have a lot of trouble. We should not be surprised when we face troubles on a daily basis. Having troubles is one of the many promises of God, but dealing with too many days' troubles at once becomes paralyzing, depressing and defeating.

I don't understand much about computers; but I do know that my computer freezes on a fairly regular basis. My computer is full of information, pictures, sermons, spreadsheets and via the Internet, the information of the entire world. However, there is only so much of this information my aging computer can take.

When too many windows are open, too many documents on the desktop, or too many pictures/videos viewed at once my computer just freezes up. There is only so much that can fit in that 3 GB of RAM.

There's only so much we can deal with at once, and Jesus says that is one day's worth. When worried, when confused, when fearful we can all at least live just the one day we have. The future plan is not always clear but we can live at least this day living for God, listening for his voice, and obeying his ways. Dr. Earl Lee, whose son was one of the Iranian hostages in 1980, speaks of finding God's peace in that fearful situation; his testimony was:

"God's will is my peace for the day…"

We may not know the entire pathway of the journey that lies before us; but we can know the next step and follow God in obedience. The God in whom we trust is *a God who is Real… a God who is Love… a God who is at Work* on our behalf. When in doubt; live for God that day… Seek his grace and strength for the challenges of this one day. Live "one day at a time." Everyone believes it but by faith we can *live* it.

Let God Be God

"Let God be God" is a rather frivolous statement – as though we have a choice in the matter. Perhaps you have stood at the table top viewpoint overlooking the Canadian Niagara Falls. The viewpoint stands literally feet from the precipice of the magnificence and power of billions of gallons of water flowing over the falls. It is an experience that brings an enveloping sense of insignificance. I have no choice but to let the great river flow. Ultimately, God will be God whether we "let" him or not.

At another level, however, we can let God be God of our lives, past, present, and future. Or we can take our lives in our own hands. Remember the foundations of faith – that are never shaken – that are always true. *God is Real ... God is Love ... And God is at Work.* The decision of faith is to trust God who is all-powerful and all-knowing – to know by faith that Jesus Christ has revealed and proved God's love toward us – and to believe in a God who is eternally at work for our benefit and blessing.

This same God gave us life. This same God who has brought us close to himself through his son Jesus Christ, is the same God who is at work in your future as well. And God does good work. He is working – his plan – which is far beyond what we could otherwise foresee. The negative, fearful, worst-case scenario expectations are unrealistic in that they factor out the workings of God.

***

I was never going to be a pastor. Not that I was negative toward the church or ministry, but I was not much of an upfront person. I didn't love to get up in front of people to draw attention to myself and certainly did not have the ability of others to get up in front of the congregation to preach. So after I made my decision as a young man to be a follower of Christ, I was still not going to be an upfront guy. Other people were so much more gifted than I.

The worst preacher the world has ever seen was used by God to confirm my call to ministry. I was a teenager in the back of the sanctuary misbehaving during church service with my good friend Dan. We would play hangman or Dan would amuse me with his amazing ability to draw cartoons of the sleeping parishioners in the back of the hymnals. Perhaps we were growing spiritually by osmosis but very slowly if that.

There was a guest preacher this particular Sunday night. I am sure he was a relative of one of the members of the local church – I am thinking a rather important member. The sermon was preceded with a duet by the guest and his wife. From our teenage perspective, being more earthly minded then spiritually good, the performance was hilarious. The soprano was screeching, the harmony was discordant, harsh and ahead of its time in an "alternative – painful music had not been invented yet" kind of way. But it was not only us. Even grown up mature church board member type people were having trouble keeping a straight face. No one could figure out if this "special" was more humorous or painful. It was a fitting introduction to the sermon.

Certainly as a teenager I was less than homiletically astute, but I could tell that the sermon was something less or at least other than sermonic. The presentation was stumbling and hesitant.

Content seemed shallow and disconnected. It seemed to me the whole congregation was very sorry for this poor "in over his head" wanna-be preacher. He didn't preach too long as I remember but it felt longer than it actually was. He concluded, sort of, in an inconclusive kind of way.

Following the sermon a song was sung and a simple invitation was given to accept Jesus Christ and become one of his followers, to live in relationship with God the Father. One after another people began to go forward, to kneel at the altar in front of the church; many of those seekers of God became Christians for the very first time. Three of those families became leaders in the church and are there to this day. All I could do at the time was to shake my head wondering what in the world was that all about?

Well fast forward four or five years. I had made a decision to be a follower of Jesus Christ. I could see no better goal for my life that to live like Jesus. I came to have a personal relationship with God through Christ which went beyond a church relationship or denominational connection. It was during this time that I began hearing/ignoring God's call to pastoral ministry. I kept saying I have never been good at that public communication stuff. Other people were so much better at being in front and leading. As one youth pastor candidate reminded me, "You don't have much of a presence... You don't exactly fill up the room when you walk through the door."

All of this made perfect sense to me as a young sociologist who had come to accept his strengths and weaknesses in life. But then God spoke. There are several times that God spoke to me in words that were almost audible ... this was one of those times. God said, "Do you remember that guy?" I thought back to the screechy scratchy duet. I was bored just thinking about the sermon. But I couldn't get over how God used that bad sermon. All I could do was shake my head and respond, "Well Lord I know that I can do that bad." And so God's working in my life has been so far beyond anything that I would have planned. A lifetime of pastoral ministry has been my calling, my joy, and has never been questioned. God always does more than we expect. But I had to let God be God, listen to his voice, obey his directions, trust him with the future.

Cheer up Someday You're Going to Die

I realize that the "Cheer up Someday You're Going to Die" advice can be proffered rather glibly to the point of insensitivity. But as people of faith, who believe that *God is Real... that God is Love...* that this *God is at Work* on our behalf; we do have a final optimism in light of eternity. Our hope in a destiny of eternal joy in the presence of Almighty God is a leap of faith. There is no way to prove the reality of heaven. But in Christ, God has sent a personal message of hope for all of his creation.

Henry Nouwen repeats the story of a World War II German prisoner who was incarcerated as a POW in a Siberian death camp. He languished in captivity, emaciated, hopelessly depressed, and finally near death. He questioned the value of life; he was ready to give up. Suddenly and unexpectedly he received a letter from his wife. It was a love letter declaring her undying devotion, reassuring him that she was waiting and hoping for his return. His spirit revived, and he found out he really did want to live. He had hope.

God has sent us a love letter when we as well feel emaciated, depressed, and wonder if it's worth it all. God's personal letter does not come with postage due but rather comes in the form of a person, his son Jesus Christ. He is real, and his words assure us of a place prepared for us that upon the conclusion of this life we will go "home." The worst-case scenario for those who live in a faith relationship with a personal, Christ-like God is to live forever in the presence of God. I don't have a good handle on what heaven/eternity looks like. I'm thinking that the biblical streets of gold are a pale, feeble attempt at understanding the reality of an eternity with God.

Jim Reeves touched on this idea with his song, '*This world is not my home*'

> "This world is not my home, I'm just a passing through
> My treasures are laid up somewhere beyond the blue
> The angels beckon me from heaven's open door
> And I can't feel at home in this world anymore."

The message of the song is surprisingly helpful theologically. This world is not our home, we are made by God and we are made for God, to be in his presence. A recent National Geographic documentary focused on life within prisons of the United States. The interviewers were touring the inmates' cells and talking to the inmates. One inmate had a kitchen all set up, a mini fridge, an easy chair; a library on the shelf, and it seemed like all the comforts of home. As the reporter poked his head in the cell the inmate had a cheery welcome, "come on in this is my home ... would you like a soda? Maybe some ice? Come on in – have a seat. The inmate was serving a fifteen year sentence and had made himself fully at home.

Another inmate had a different attitude. His cell looks like an empty shell. A cot-like bed, a hard stool, a desk, small shelf and a stainless steel sink and toilet. This isn't where I live, he tells the interviewer, this is my dwelling place for little while. This is just transitory. When I get out of here I will be in a better place.

In a way we are imprisoned in a physical body, in a fallen world, with the deepest desire for something better. The pain, the struggles, the injustices, the regrets, are all part of the tapestry of life woven in along with the love, joy, faith and hope of life. The circumstances of our lives, in a way we don't fully understand, are part of a preparation for the life to come.

So the bad news is that this ain't heaven yet (although by faith the news is never all bad). The good news is there is a limit to this less than heavenly existence. We are filled with hope that an infinite God is love - eternally. We live our lives based on the certainty that, just as we have lived our lives in relationship with God in this life; we will also live in relationship with him for all eternity. As the psalmist says, "in his presence there is fullness of joy."

Live for Today – Long for Eternity

CONCLUSION

Life Will Shake You Up

For the past several years, we have driven older cars. The hope is that these stalwart vehicles will last at least until my daughter graduates from college. My mechanic has recommended that we use synthetic oil. Synthetic oil is manufactured to perfection; the molecules or particles or whatever components that make this "oil" are perfectly symmetrical. As a result they provide near-perfect lubrication. Machinery runs much more smoothly on this artificial "stuff."

The oil that eventually becomes basic 10W/40 engine oil is a much less predictable process. Various kinds of animal bones, vegetation, dinosaurs, and who knows what else are compressed deep beneath the earth and after a certain number of millions of years are reduced to the liquid carbon type stuff we call oil. This oil however, is less than perfect; its molecules and components are not perfectly symmetrical. It does not function as perfectly as the artificial; but it is real oil.

We are created to live real life. Real life is not neat, clean, and predictable. Life is not neat. As Rabbi Kushner says, "Why can't we let the universe have a few rough edges?" *(When Bad Things Happen to Good People)* Our world is not a clock that has been wound and left to run on its own. Reality is not perfectly symmetrical. Pain, disease, injustice, and tragedy seem to intrude their way into our lives with little rhyme or reason.

Face the Facts ... there are times when life shakes us up.

We Will Never Know All Things

In our humanity, however, we want every aspect of life to make sense. The principle of cause and effect are ingrained into our psyche as educated Western materialists. We not only want every effect to have cause; we also want a full understanding of the cause, meaning, and purpose of the troubling, painful, and perhaps undeserved events of life.

It is obvious that we will never understand every event of life fully. But even though we know this, when it comes to our personal suffering and pain, we act as though we should understand all about it. Our faith tells us that we will one day understand in the life to come. But I somehow think that even in eternity we will have something less than a God like understanding of all there is.

Are we willing to let God be God? Can we accept our humanity and the limits of our knowledge and perception of those things that are eternal and mysterious? I believe there are those things that happen as a result of God's providential intervention in our lives. I also believe that there are those things that happen just because we live in a world that is not totally predictable. Some things just happen and through it all God is at work for our help and for his glory. Other things happen as a consequence of our personal decisions. Still others happen because of the decisions of others that affect us indirectly. Sometimes it's not hard to tell the reasons behind the events of our lives. Other times it is much more difficult. Quite often, perhaps most often, we can't figure it out. An indispensable step towards serenity and peace is the acceptance of our humanity and the limits of our understanding. The rest is up to God.

Our Faith Foundation Never Changes

And so the events of life often come unexpectedly and cruelly. They cause us pain; they shake our lives. Life is an ever changing challenge. But there are those things that never change. It is vital that as we face that which is so hard to comprehend, that we do not lose sight of those things we do understand and believe in faith.

As Christians we believe that there really is a God. It is obvious to us that there is some awesome transcendent creator God who has made all things. We also believe that God is a loving

151

benevolent God. We have come to be reconciled to this God through his son Jesus Christ. We have come to know the spirit and character of this personal God. We believe that God is love. We finally believe that God is at work in our world for our strength, guidance, and serenity. It is the witness of Scripture, the testimony of the Saints of the church, and our personal experience that God is an active, loving, caring and helping God.

These foundation stones of our faith will never change. And upon this foundation we are able to stand firmly in response to the crises of life with purpose, strength, and with the help of Almighty God himself.

The Choice Is Ours

Rabbi Harold S Kushner writes further "The question we should be asking is not, 'Why did this happen to me? What did I do to deserve this?' That is really an unanswerable pointless question. Better question would be 'now that this has happened to me, what am I going to do about it?'" *(When Bad Things Happen To Good People)*

The premise of this book is that Christians really can choose to respond by faith when the unexpected crises and tragedies threaten to shake and shatter our lives. I have an incurable disease. The choices were there: self-pity, blame, bitterness, depression but somehow by God's grace:

"My faith has found resting place, Not in device or creed; I trust the ever living one his wounds for me shall plead. I need no other argument; I need no other plea; It is enough that Jesus died, And that he died for me." *(My Faith Has Found a Resting Place – Hewitt 1891)*

My hope and prayer is that God's faithfulness in my life will be an encouragement and challenge that will lead others to make a faith decision in the crisis time of their lives. I encourage you to use the five aspects presented here as a guide in purposefully responding with faith to a personal God who loves you with an everlasting love.

The Ardrey family shortly following Ken's diagnosis.

REFERENCES

Barry, John M. *The Great Influenza*. New York: Penguin Books, 1947.

Chambers, Oswald, Edited by James Reimann. *My Utmost for His Highest*. Grand Rapids: Discovery House Publishers, 1992.

Colson, Charles. *Loving God*. Grand Rapids: Zondervan Publishing House, 1987.

Floyd, Wayne Whitson. *The Wisdom and Witness of Dietrich Bonhoeffer*. Minneapolis: Fortress Press, 2000.

Fox, Michael J. *Always Looking Up: The Adventures of an Incurable Optimist.*. New York: Hyperion, 2009.

Lucky Man: a memoir. New York: Hyperion, 2002.

Jethani, Skye. *The Divine Commodity: Discovering a Faith Beyond Consumer Christianity*. Grand Rapids: Zondervan Publishing House, 2009.

Jonas, Robert A. *Henri Nouwen*. Mayknoll, NY: Orbis Books, 1999.

Kubler-Ross, Elizabeth. *On Death and Dying*. NewYork: Scribner, 1969.

Kushner, Harold S. *When Bad Things Happen to Good People*. New York: Anchor Books, 1981.

Nouwen, Henri *The Return of the Prodigal Son*. New York: Image, 1993.

Here and Now. New York: Crossroad, 1994.

The Inner Voice of Love. New York: Doubleday, 1996.

Paul S. Dayhoff. *Living Stones in Africa: Pioneers of the Church of the Nazarene.* Kansas City: Nazarene Publishing House, 1999.

Phelps, Richard. *Undertaker's Son.* Guilford, CT: Lyons Press, 2007.

Six die from brain-eating amoeba after swimming. Associated Press as reported on www.msnbc.msn.com, 9/28/2007.

Ten Boom, Corrie. *The Hiding Place.* New York: Bantam Books. 1971.

Wesley, John. *Wesley's Journal.* Kansas City: Beacon Hill Press. Reprinted 1978.

Willard, Dallas. *Hearing God.* Downers Grove, IL: Intervarsity Press, 1999. Page 46